WOMEN IN A
STRANGE LAND

WOMEN IN A STRANGE LAND

Search for a New Image

Edited by
CLARE BENEDICKS FISCHER,
BETSY BRENNEMAN,
and
ANNE McGREW BENNETT

FORTRESS PRESS   Philadelphia

Library of Congress Catalog Card Number 74-26326

ISBN 0-8006-1204-3

4626J74   Printed in U.S.A.   1-1204

By the rivers of Babylon,
  there we sat down, yea,
  we wept,
when we remembered Zion.

We hanged our harps upon the willows
  in the midst thereof.

For there they that carried us away captive
  required of us a song;
and they that wasted us
  required of us mirth, saying,
  Sing us one of the songs of Zion.

How shall we sing the Lord's song
  in a strange land?

                    Psalm 137:1-4 (AV)

Contents

Foreword

In recent years, the women's movement has lifted up the issues that women in our society must struggle with if they are to find opportunity to grow toward wholeness. Through the dialogue and actions of the movement, church-related women have felt a stimulus and excitement as they have found their own unique task and have entered into it. Some women in the church have become aware of the ways in which biblical and theological teachings over the centuries have contributed to and reinforced the limitations placed on women. Having come to this awareness (which was not completely new for many), not all women have felt that they could remain within the tradition which they now see as dehumanizing to them. In the pages which follow you will find the words of women who have chosen to maintain some form of relationship and commitment to the institutional church. Having done so, they, like all women who are making this decision, find themselves with questions to ask and problems to solve.

These women have seen their task, as part of the church, to explore and challenge traditional theology. But more importantly, women who continue to relate to the church have also begun to develop their own forms of theologizing, in which a major premise is to take very seriously the way in which means and ends intertwine. In the course of this exploration and creativity, women have entered into communal theologizing based on their experience as women and the results have been not only traditional papers, books, and lectures, but also shared experiences, new forms of thinking and talking together, in a movement toward new theological understandings and in the context of a sense of the Spirit's presence in their midst.

So it is important that this book has been created through the kind of communal process that women have been developing.

It is appropriate to a pluralistic time in which varied histories and experiences are bringing us to new understandings which must interact with each other. Such theologizing will continue, for there is much yet to be explored and much to be redirected into fresh ways if women everywhere are really to enter into the wholeness of life which the gospel holds out for all people. Theologizing by women must continue as a distinct piece of the church's activities until it is truly taken seriously as part of the total stream of the church's life.

The writings here brought together represent a sharing of insights and experiences by this particular group of women. They will be helpful to other women who are caught up in the same search because the issues and ideas are common to us all. Just as importantly, however, the collection has something to say to men as well. Its contents should be carefully considered by all who presume to teach, preach, or direct the affairs of the church. These chapters will contribute to a deeper understanding of the more than half the church's membership that is women. More importantly, they will help in opening up new knowledge of the Spirit's movement in our day.

Claire Randall

Introduction

Women who for untold centuries have
been separated from each other are coming together—talking
and listening to one another. Women are finding that they are
not alone either in their dreams of what life might mean, or in
their experiences of being denied access even to an opportunity to work to fulfill their dreams.

Our hope for this collection of writings has been to encourage
the communication of ideas and feelings among women concerned about liberation and the church. We believe that
women who share this particular concern need to hear themselves and that this attentiveness gives confidence and
deepens the exchange of experiences. At first the voices may
sound self-contained but, as women speak for themselves, the
voices resonate and touch a varied audience of women who
seemingly share little. There seem to be no prerequisites for
the sharing of common disability and hope. To the extent that
these women speak to and for others (those who know what is
being said but have yet to articulate it themselves) they become
representatives of a larger community of women who meet only
through the written word. *Women in a Strange Land* is directed
to this ever-expanding dialogue.

A group of women connected with the Graduate Theological
Union[1] in Berkeley, California, have been working in
churches, in secular society, and in seminaries toward an exchange of ideas and hopes for the church and theology in
relation to woman's liberation. This book has grown out of that

1. The Graduate Theological Union is a twelve-year-old educational consor-
tium made up of nine seminaries (six Protestant, three Catholic), and various
agencies including the Center for Judaic Studies, Center for Urban Black
Studies, and Institute of Lay Theology/School of Applied Theology. The
G.T.U. also works cooperatively with the Graduate Division of the University
of California, Berkeley.

1

experience which has, as common ground, the Office of Women's Affairs of the G.T.U., created in 1970 for community among the women of graduate and seminary schools. Some of the contributors have routine contact through classroom and academic involvement; others have been associated with the programs of the Office.

The several chapters and writers reflect the strengths and weaknesses of theological education for women today. Although the volume expresses an ecumenical collaboration of Protestant and Catholic, there are no Jewish voices. Although the contributors vary in age and activity from seminary students to young professionals to women whose chronological years belie their tireless involvement in institutional and theological work, there are no black women, third-world women, or working-class women speaking here. These voices are not heard because they are barely present in the seminary community—a reflection of social conditioning and operative admission and recruitment policies. We continue to work for the day when this disproportionate "silence" will be broken. Three of our contributors extend the geographic scope: Claire Randall, Nelle Morton, and Dorothee Soelle. The first two have visited Berkeley and served as important models for the women here. The third, a German theologian, met with several women from the G.T.U. when she spoke at an international religious conference in California a few years ago.

The book is about change and movement; about a certain kind of being in a certain place taking steps, even leaps, and arriving a different, better being in a different, better place. Content and format are interrelated: the book is about process and the book *is* process. Part One begins with the questing self, unsure of who it is but convinced that something is not right. There is alienation, disunion, estrangement, a feeling of being handicapped by incompleteness—a bleak picture—but this awareness is the crucial first step enabling the search to begin. Several viewpoints are included on this dawning of consciousness and its implications for woman's identity as seminary student, single parent, young single woman, and wife. It shows

the self asking, "Who am I *really*?" and then exploring
—moving forward, getting bruised, never quite sure of its direction but determined to see what wholeness can be and to
reject what it is not.

Movement from new awareness implies activity. Part Two
explores the way women have moved beyond recognition of
the incomplete self to building a complete one. It shows
women doing, working hard, carving out new ways, exploring
new forms of "ministry." Implicit is the sense that developing
the complete self can be done only in relationship to other
persons, institutions, and communities. Two women widen
their understanding of ministry through peace activism; a
woman minister shares her experience in a woman-man parish
team ministry; a woman scholar functions within the male-
dominated field of Christian ethics—she is shown doing ethics;
in relating to her Catholic community a suburban wife and
mother advances a new concept of the Virgin Mary; and a
seminary student seeks ordination and envisions her ministry
while doing it.

In Part Three the self claims its wholeness—its vision of full
personhood. Women, still being made more aware, still working hard, are now moving beyond the self toward the implications of full personhood for the community of women and
the entire human family. From the diversity of viewpoints
comes a unifying push toward what we can be together. Dorothee Soelle offers one perspective and her translator, an
American/German feminist, responds to what she has translated; a woman scholar challenges the normative concept of
Christian ministry; two women use the tools of biblical and
sociological scholarship to confront traditional theological understandings and the new awareness of women. Part Three
begins with a meditation on liturgy and comes to an end with a
speculation on "what celebration could be . . . were the oppressed of the earth trusted to become a valid part of that
community."

There is, finally, the sense that, through the processes of
self-searching and working, great changes are taking place em-

powering us to envision new images and proclaim new possibilities for theology, for the church, for women, for all people.

Clare Benedicks Fischer, Betsy Brenneman,
     Anne McGrew Bennett

PART ONE:
WHO ARE WE?

1.

. . . a part of me
is missing

Where is "me"
a part of me is missing
aborted—still born—
    since that Garden time

    yet, without plan or warning
    ever and ever again moving
    deep within my body
      and soul
    a person   "image of God"
      WOMAN
    comes gasping, grasping
    for the breath of life
    struggling to be born
    and live—free

pushed back, covered over by
myriad words—intoned word
    you are not man
    you are woman
    created for a man's pleasure
      and comfort
    created to bear man-child
      to rule you
    created to bear woman-child
      to be subject to man-child

Man-child, oh man-child
my father, husband, brothers, sons

do you feel a deep stirring,
  rebellion
at the intoned word for you?
  You are man, be big
  be strong, powerful
  never surrender: succeed
  let no tears break through
  be mind, not heart
      heart is for the weak
  be arrogant–aggressive

CRY, CRY BELOVED IMAGE
Who calls us both?

—Anne McGrew Bennett, April 1972

2.

Woman to Woman: Finding the Self

KATHLEEN BREWER

A friend recently shared a story with me that reveals, I think, where a number of women are regarding that vague word, "selfhood." This friend was sitting in a circle of women in a workshop. One of the beginning exercises in the group was to go around the circle, each woman introducing herself to the group *without* describing herself in either of the relational roles of wife or mother. One of the women there, my friend told me, burst into tears when it was her turn to speak —she had realized that, aside from being "somebody's wife" and "somebody's mother," she didn't have anything to "say for herself."

That woman was grappling with a serious issue that faces all of us as women. She was reaching for a sense of *selfhood*. Selfhood—the sense of being autonomous and responsible in one's decision-making, the felt possibility of making, even changing, history, the personal responsibility for life's meaning—is often denied persons in our present culture, but it has rarely ever been a possibility for women.

The messages we receive about our value and worth as selves come from people or groups of people with whom we interact: school teachers, parents and family, advertising, images flashed on the TV and movie screen. Messages about how worthy we are come also from the things we *don't* see on TV: women as great heroines instead of temptresses; women leaving men because the future calls, rather than the opposite; women risking their lives for a goal, rather than fleeing and spraining their ankles on the way. All these images of women provide us with clues as to what we are and should be.

9

I can recall situations in my own childhood and adolescence—and even in recent months—which show me how precarious my own selfhood as a woman has been in our culture. I recall the incredible pain during adolescence when I was a wallflower at dances, while all the girls with breasts seemed to be dancing a lot. For some reason, I wasn't "worth" being with. I can recall planning to become a teacher—as most women in my family did—"just in case" (i.e., just in case I didn't find a husband). Everyone said it was something I could "fall back on." I wonder now how much my life, and the lives of other women, have been lived, in a sense, by omission, with no plans for a future but with non-plans of things to "fall back on," "just in case."

I invite you to think back on your life, to remember times in which you received messages about how important you, as a person, were. All of us have messages: perhaps pressure from dates to "prove your love"; perhaps getting turned down for a scholarship because "women get married and aren't worth the investment"; or perhaps simply being ignored, or greeted with amusement, when you expressed your views in a group.

So how do we become selves? How do we get from that place of feeling resentful, vaguely in pain, and absolutely *certain* that we could never get that job or master the income tax form—to moving with assurance in social situations, liking and trusting our abilities and feeling okay about our need to learn more? The difference that selfhood makes is the difference between feeling as if someone or something else is running our lives, and feeling that we ourselves are "in charge." It's the difference that freedom makes: freedom to make and to follow through on decisions, freedom to say yes and to say no.

In our present culture, a major clue to selfhood for women is found in exactly the place where previously our destruction has been: in groups of people, and in individual persons, to whom we relate. We are presently surrounded by groups and messages that urge us not to risk and grow. We need to develop and create groups that not only help us realize just how important and creative and courageous we are, but that also help us gain skills and confidence to act on our abilities. We need to stop spending so much time absorbed in things that teach us "noselfness" and get in touch with things and people who will help us up the road to selfhood.

Where, O where, is this paradise? In the home of your neighbor down the street on Wednesday nights. In dorm lounges in colleges across the country. In the parlors of "old" women in quiet neighborhoods. In the women's classes in churches and synagogues. In the coffee lounges of corporations, where secretaries take their breaks. The paradise (which we create) is in women's groups or "consciousness-raising" groups, as they are often called. These groups are gatherings of women who range from being angry about the oppression of women to being distrustful of the women's movement, who are divorcées, mothers, professional women, widows, and retired women, artists, writers, clergy —as varied and uniquely interesting as women themselves truly are. What is happening in these groups is that women who want to be selves are gathering together, seeking other women with whom to relate on an ongoing basis, and struggling to uncover their sense of integrity after years of denying it.

The groups take various forms and directions, depending on the stage of growth of the women who form them. Some groups are informal, meet weekly or twice a month, and are simply support groups where women share their lives and daily struggles and decisions. Other groups are task-oriented, such as those directed toward political action or toward development of skills (writers' collectives, poets' guilds, self-help health care). Still others are support groups for professional women, or for women in a specific situation (young mothers, women in menopause, students in law school). Because there is no outside standard to meet, group goals and methods are set by the women themselves. Even becoming a member, then, entails an exploration of the self: "What *do* I want?" Slowly, women begin to uncover their needs and desires for their lives. The group nourishes, challenges, and consolidates their personal power to accomplish these goals.

One group of struggling selves of which I was a member developed among women enrolled in graduate professional programs at the Graduate Theological Union in Berkeley. All of these women were planning to enter the professional ministry, and our denominations varied: Unitarian, Lutheran, Disciples of Christ, Presbyterian, and United Church of Christ. Most of us had entered seminary before the more "liberal" schools began opening up their rolls to significant numbers of women. Each of us had begun by being the only female in an entire classroom of male students, and had been struggling for at least two years with male-dominated dynamics which pretended we weren't there ("Now, class, when you're ministers and have a wife and family . . ."). Some of us had a gnawing sense that the theology we were learning was at odds with our experience as women; we wondered constantly if we were unchristian, unfit for ministry. At times, all the outward signs seemed to indicate so! All of us were carrying full academic loads, most of us had part-time jobs or a field education position, and three of the seven of us were married.

The group developed out of an evening's discussion at the G.T.U. Women's Center about sexuality. Because most of us were friends or at least knew each other, and because, as we discovered later, our lives were so hectic and tinged with desperation, we decided to gather at the Center for a potluck dinner once a week. The purpose of our sessions was simply to *be together*, to relax and enjoy each other.

Our culture usually equates something as serious-sounding as "becoming a self" with "going it alone," the kind of rugged individualism in which a person decides that being a self means being apart from others who might in any way infringe on one or define one's self. Not only is this impossible, but for women, much of our struggle has been *because* we are separated from each other. In our suburbs, each woman has her own home, her own appliances; there are few ways to meet with other women and so each of us has had to struggle with her feelings all alone. In seminary, we were similarly isolated: there were only two or three of us in each seminary; we rarely saw each other, or experienced a sense of having women as friends. Thus, for most of us, the *acceptance* available in the group was a significant factor in our becoming more aware and confident in ourselves and in our sense of reality.

"I needed to be with other women who were doing what I was doing professionally and who could support me in a professional sense . . . my experience as a woman in seminary was validated and I didn't feel so peculiar and strange."

"At seminary I was seen as the 'resident feminist.' I had been trying to 'turn on' seminary women to the movement . . . but this was a group that was already concerned! I wanted, and found, a group where I could relax."

"People at seminary, mostly men, were always addressing me, indirectly or directly, with the question, 'What are *you* doing here?' No one ever asked me that in this group. I was accepted."

For several of the women, entering a women's group was a considerable risk—not all were sure they even *liked* "being with women" and others had had miserable experiences in encounter groups. However, we seemed to develop a level of trust which gave us a new insight into what a communal group situation could be like.

"I generally hate group situations. I'm better on a one-to-one kind of relating. Group situations for me will now be with women or not at all. I've found that I can be more honest and get down to gut-level experiences, once I'm away from men-women games. Contrary to what most people seem to think, I find that women together play fewer games than men and women do."

"I'm suspicious of encounter groups. I'd have had to defend myself in an encounter group—men would have been asking me what I meant and I didn't *know* exactly what I meant. In our group I didn't need to articulate how deep my pain was—all I had to do was grow."

During the course of our weekly dinners together—often marked by one woman or another pouring out her doubts about a relationship, about herself as a minister, or her struggles with school—many of the women in the group began to trust their experience and to heed their personal sense of direction.

"I gradually saw my own experience speaking to more universal things, such as sexism in general. When we were together, I realized that what people called *my* problems weren't just mine. I grew more self-confident."

As the women began to discover that each self had real life experiences to share and, moreover, had striking commonality with other selves present, a real respect and caring for each person in the group developed.

"Every woman there was so unique and significant in her own way. The group really destroyed the myth that women are boring or frivolous!"

One woman felt a new sense of trust and began to realize that she could, without embarrassment, really choose the company of women because it was meaningful to her.

"There was a fairly incredible amount of trust in this group— I'm not sure why . . . there was trust in people's confidence with personal matters. I haven't ever had quite that level of trust with any group."

"One thing is beginning to happen with me, especially coming out of my relationships with women—and that is the need to identify and accept caring feelings about women. Being able to say, 'I really care about women.'"

Because the group was a student group, it dissolved purposely in June after six months of weekly meetings. Since that time, several women have reflected on the strength and weaknesses of the group.

"By June, I was beginning to experience some frustration with the group meetings. We had pushed our limits as a group and my needs were changing."

"When we were gathering together, we were almost too supportive, I think. Looking back, I see that we were in some ways unwilling to challenge each other on certain issues because the ground we were on was so fragile. We thought it might disappear."

"Most of us had been immersed daily in repeated experiences of being foreign or being rejected. I don't think that I could have handled it if people had expressed their inability to understand certain things."

"I desperately needed someone to say yes to me."

After our six months' time together most felt ready to end the group. The freedom to stand apart from the group, to critique it, had been found by these women whose selves had grown and were sustained through their intensely demanding seminary experiences. New confidence led us into new situations and our needs changed. Said one graduate, "Now, I'd like to develop a support group for professional women in the church —people who are having to strategize, people with whom I can share more of the specifics of my profession."

Most of the women in our group have, since our final meal together, become members of other support groups which fit their interests and needs. Two attend a women's prayer group; others have developed a class on women's autobiography; still others occasionally attend a "woman's ingathering," roughly analogous to a feminist church. Said one woman who was a member of the women's class, "As women feel more confident in their ability to articulate, their discoveries about life are really mind-blowing!"

While the group members I interviewed did not necessarily see membership in a women's group as a necessary aspect of their lives on an ongoing basis, all are now involved in the women's movement in one form or another, and all agreed that the support among women had been crucial to them. All of us are proceeding to the next phase of our lives: some are working in church internships, one is in Japan teaching, some are publishing a booklet of papers produced by a women's class, several are now employed by the Office of Women's Affairs at the G.T.U. I think that each of us, in her own way, began to discover in that group an immense, untapped power in selfhood.

I myself envision a life in which, as a matter of priority, I am in extensive contact with women. Although I am lucky to be in a marriage relationship with a man who is very supportive and growing and loving, I find there is a certain kind of "free space" I feel in women's consciousness-raising groups that keeps my self intact in a world which is still predicated on the exclusion and "no-self-ness" of women. I find a great sense of life and possibility in a good women's group, in contrast to the frustration I find in most male-dominated structures. This year, my group-contact with women has come in the form of two seminary classes—one exploring the history of mother-goddess cults and their implications, one studying women's autobiog-

raphies. In addition, I have found a truly good friend who is a
woman. It is clear to me that these things, when added to the
growing I was doing last year in our seminary women's group,
have really helped me turn the corner of my own selfhood. The
"signals" of becoming a self are difficult to define, but let me
at least mention some that I perceive in my own life:

I decided that I could be a minister because I am skilled,
compassionate, and human. No one, during my entire stay at
seminary, ever told me this.

I decided I could write a master's thesis because I am intelligent and because my experience is important. And then I
wrote it.

I started taking an art class, something I always "wanted" to
do but never quite "got around to." I found out that I can draw.

I don't laugh so much at things that aren't funny.

Just recently, I noticed that I wasn't scared about speaking
before groups—my stomach doesn't get tight and my voice
squeaky, as they once did—and that I can walk into a group of
strangers without acting strange myself.

These things are not ends in themselves, but they have indicated to me how my life has been changing from fearful and
passive to outgoing, realistic, and responsibly active. I find that
my marriage has improved as I have become more myself: my
husband seems more relaxed; I'm giving *him* a little more
psychic and emotional space as I give myself the same. Another
thing: I feel that my sexuality is becoming more well-rounded,
more full and trustworthy, the more I like and respect and take
care of myself as a creative person.

What is absolutely critical here, in my estimation, is that I did
not develop this way alone. I find that, when I falter, I need
other women to confirm my creativity in a world which generally negates it. For me, selfhood has been and still is an ongoing
process of exploring my growth and potential as a woman with
other women. The first critical step was that of entering into a
women's group. That began a development toward a fullness of
life that I might have missed, were it not for the women's
movement and the concomitant movement of women I know
toward full life.

3.

Dancing Life Anew

JACQUELINE MEADOWS

I am a minister, a dancer, and a single parent. Through these roles, within a parish setting, I hope to communicate the Christian message of personal and societal liberation from sin and death. I feel called to the ministry of dance as liturgy, social criticism, recreation, and therapy to facilitate a holistic response to the Christian message of liberation. In my journey toward this ministry, I have moved from vagueness to clarity toward wholeness. Theologically, I have actualized the theme of death and resurrection as I have traveled through loneliness, pain, rootlessness, and alienation.

The journey began seventeen years ago when I was in seminary, working on a master of arts degree in Christian Education. I was in a state of depression. I could not sleep, I was lonely and helpless to identify what was happening inside of me. Symbolically, my life was a bunch of lines. The lines revealed how I experienced life and God. The lines were vertical, horizontal, and were broken. They ran parallel, were uneven and staggered. The lines inside me did not meet to form squares, rectangles, triangles, or octagons. In primary relationships, especially male-female communication, my lines never met others to design circles or spirals. The configurations were tense, oppositional, paradoxical, and partitional. Integration did not happen inside and equality was not present in male-female sexuality, so real intimacy did not emerge. Although my commitment to minister through the roles which I had chosen was deep and enthusiastic, a part of me was missing.

I could not ask for help—I did not know what help was needed. Now I know that I was struggling with the discrepancy between who I was and who I wanted to be. Intuitively I knew

17

that I had not fulfilled my potential as a female person. There was a self hiding in the shadows and evading definition. The self of intensity, energy, and creativity wanted to break forth into my conscious awareness and be affirmed, by myself and by the world, as part of my identity. I was defensive, insecure, fragmented, and at my core wanted integration and inter-relatedness with others as equals.

Intellectually, God was totally other, demanding and untouchable. God was good, perfect, complete, and masculine. God was at the pinnacle of life's hierarchy. His place and "Godness" was maintained by the godlessness of persons who were deprived, fallen, self-abased, evil, and especially as female persons, alienated. The biblical "blessing" on women as secondary, helpmate, and subordinate stifled any motivation which I might have had to fulfill my commitment to become a minister. My theological stance glossed over the reality of the struggle going on inside me. My conditioning by church and society, coupled with my own self-abasement, blocked me from being totally touched by the reality of God's confrontation.

I did not see, as I do now, that through struggle, beginnings and movements were being made in the direction of unification and wholeness. There *were* lines in me that flowed out to make a few half-circles, semispirals, partial squares, and broken triangles. God was dancing in the lines and prodding me, in my depression, to apprehend the totality of myself and the mutuality, interrelatedness, reciprocity, and spontaneity of life. Yahweh-Elohim was calling me to get myself together in God-creation so that my worship of God would not be short-circuited and I would not manipulate those to whom I wished to minister. I did not know then that God was moving, piercing my complacency and sadness, urging me to dissolve the discrepancy between who I was and who I was created to be. I did not know, so I chose to negate the call, believing that I was affirming God by enlarging a man I had created in God's image. I got as close as I could to professional ministry by training to be a religious educator and by marrying a minister.

We went into ministry together, committing ourselves to the

institutional church and all that went with it: right belief, ethical behavior, fidelity, role expectations, and hard work. The churches and communities where we served got two for the price of one. We were glued together by commitment to realities outside ourselves. The roles which we played were dehumanizing for others as well as ourselves when the energy poured into those outside commitments was the only source of our self-worth. I gave profusely of my time, energy, and creativity, yet did not value those personal sacrifices which I made. I "did it for him" and saw myself as contingent, instrumental, and accidental.

Sacrifice of the self for someone or for a cause is an essential ingredient of my Christian faith. But only when one really knows her/his needs and desires can one freely sacrifice them for others. To give up something without knowing or experiencing its value is "cheap grace," to use Bonhoeffer's words. I defined myself by the image of another and ignored *my* responsibility to develop personally and socially toward creation in God's image. Neither history nor society encourages women to risk being responsible for self-growth and self-identity. To give my "all" to my marriage and my husband's ministry while not psychically whole, was to give manipulatively and seductively—I expected others to fill the vacuum of my self-identity. When the relationship came under severe strain, there was not enough of "me" to sustain me. I faced an agonizing loneliness that had been coated over by marriage, and I felt accumulated anger and hurt. When separation came, I was rootless. As a woman I had not been prepared to feel purposeful, valuable, and autonomous while uncoupled.

Divorce is brokenness. (When I say divorce I mean all those experiences leading up to and following the legal ritual that terminates marriage.) For me, however, the brokenness was both destructive and redemptive. The theological precepts that had immobilized movement toward wholeness in seminary proved to be an anchor as my marriage collapsed and I moved from wifehood to womanhood. This crisis renewed, redefined, filled, and expanded the old concepts with new meaning. Emo-

tionally, for the first time in my life I understood death, resurrection, and new life. The "word became flesh." I died, partly
by circumstance and partly by choice, to the roles that had
defined me. Also, I came to understand those concepts on a
societal level: the awakening to the nature of my own existence
intensified my identity with the oppressed in their struggles for
liberation.

Divorce has made me a single parent. I have tried to maintain
the delicate balance between the need for community, the
demand of parental responsibilities, and the imperative to
grow, but I'm not always successful and can easily feel guilt,
shame, or blame if I do not measure up to society's myth of
perfect parenthood. The other side of the picture is our new
community—three children and I face each other as persons.
We have been "birthed" together out of chaos and have been
sensitized to each other in a new way. As we recognize, respect,
and respond to one another, we hurt and we heal. We are doing
a better job of helping each other to actualize our individual
potential and we are less obsessed with role perfection. The
right of the children to struggle for their own autonomy, to have
privacy and to develop independence, has naturally been encouraged by single parenthood.

There is pain too. I am geographically separated from my
oldest son and see him only six weeks a year. The separation
makes impossible a continual nurturing of the responsiveness,
stimulation, touching, affection, and aliveness that passes between us when we are together. I am forever scared by that
broken, sacred relatedness. I live with the fear, in the pit of my
stomach, that he will reject me. The miracle is that he still gives
me the gift of responsiveness.

Through divorce, I've discovered that I'm alone. Sexual
union temporarily removed that aloneness, but sexual intimacy
reaches its most profound expression only when it emerges out
of a *social* intercourse between two autonomous individuals. I
left my marriage because I did not feel loved for who I was and
because I did not love myself. I was not autonomous. I keep
alive the trembling hope that I will be able to commit myself to
a relationship in which both of us will profoundly recognize,

respect, and respond to the intellect, spirit, emotions, and body of the other. Out of a recognition of who we are and are not, we will receive and give each other nurture. I am not yet whole enough or strong enough for such a commitment.

The brokenness of divorce also brought forth dance from the neglected core of my being. Shortly after the birth of my fourth child, I went into a frightening state of depression. My husband was gone and I was left with four children, two of them in diapers. It seemed that the tears would never stop. My depression was similar to what I had experienced at seminary, except that then it was impulsed entirely from within. This time external pressures met the pressures from inside and I felt crushed. I had given of myself more than I had taken into myself. Mistakenly, I thought that I had attained my goal to communicate love of God and love of neighbor, and to strive for completeness as wife, mother, community leader, and religious educator, but I had ignored the religious injunction to love God and neighbor through wholeness. So one more child was waiting within to be born—the dancing, creative, artistic child. My state of depression was the contraction which brought this child forth from my center. The child I had ignored in seminary and marriage was tired of being hidden. The new life cried out for recognition and nurture, so I enrolled in modern and jazz dance classes at a nearby college. The new child also needed to meet and interrelate with theology, so I returned to ministry with reaffirmed commitment.

When the conjunction of aloneness and new hope could no longer be ignored, I acted on behalf of my own salvation and chose the seminary to be my home during a time of exile. I knew that the struggles begun years ago in seminary were still with me, dangling like hot wires inside of me, and the spirit and energy still coursing through those wires shocked and pained me when I touched them again. But I also remembered that the seminary community had provided a deep experience of communion, creativity, and growth, so I began to connect those wires again, in the same environment, for a new source of energy in ministry.

Now, that which relates theology, movement, and ministry

for me is dance. Dance is my configuration, the design that affects me and which I in turn affect; it is my movement in the *world*. Dance is the inner self of intensity, spirituality, sexuality, intuition, energy, and emotion that was waiting to be released seventeen years earlier. The nonintellectual self is in creative tension with the theological self as I minister through dance. Now permission has been granted, the risk taken, support given for the integration of heart, soul, mind, and strength with others who are struggling for mutuality and completeness. The dance goes on in God, in whom we move and have our being.

I know now what I did not know then—that I live in a culture in which humanity is separated and yet bound together by depravity, by our neediness, whether it be emotional, spiritual, or physical. To deny that neediness or that boundness is to ignore and fail to nurture the sacred thread that ties us together. The radical steps which I have taken to discover my own identity have sensitized me to others. I have an awareness now that I did not have then—God is present to me in my radical act of freedom, in my choice—now for the first time in my life—to take responsibility for myself.

Now, as a minister, dancer, and single parent I move, despite and because of depravity, to celebrate myself, my life, and my hope in a revolving, spinning, changing world. This is the process by which I actualize God's call to help in the fulfillment of creation. It is my religious process, my movement between the world and myself, between giving and receiving, between past and present (becoming future), between feeling and intellect, between creativity and role expectation, between pain and joy, in the context, culture, and configuration of my life.

4.

Single and Whole

KATHY JAN JOHNSON

Who are we, the single women? We are the continually increasing numbers of divorced, widowed, unmated, and by choice single women. Statistics show that there are over fourteen million women in the United States who are classified as being without husbands. Over nine million of them are widows, two million are divorcées or separated from their husbands, and over three million have never married.[1] As the number of single women increases, so do their concerns and needs. Yet society has done little in the way of creating or supporting a positive image of the single woman. As a consequence, few of us have realized the opportunities and possibilities in living a single life.

The single woman lives in a society that revolves around the nuclear family. There are family rates on planes and trains, family nights at restaurants, and family picnics. It is even difficult to go to a grocery store and buy just a half-dozen eggs. Certainly the family needs support and occasions for togetherness in our fast-moving world, but what is there for the rest of us, the millions of single persons, and particularly for the single woman who lives in this same world? What does our society offer me other than destructive myths that build an image of me as half-person, unfulfilled?

If a young woman has chosen to be single, she is looked on with suspicion or pity. At age thirty, or even before, she is already called a "career woman." If she is over thirty-five, she is an "old maid" or "spinster." Her sexuality (or lack thereof) is of course in question. It is assumed that she could not "get her man" or that she must care for a sickly relative.

1. Isabella Taves, *Women Alone* (New York: Funk and Wagnalls, 1968), p. 13.

The divorced woman has a different problem. She is often perceived as a threat, particularly to married women (even to church women who find their husbands serving on the board with her). Young or old, the divorced woman is often felt to be on the hunt for another husband. The divorce rate increased 80 percent from 1960 to 1970; that means an increased number of divorced women with special concerns: raising children, legal problems, financial struggles, and on top of those, the burdens imposed on her by the negative attitudes of others. She is sometimes given sympathy, occasionally even positive encouragement, but more often than not she is cast aside as having made a mistake or perpetrated evil.

The widowed woman, particularly in her older years, receives the most pity: she has lost all that she ever "lived for." Nonetheless, she ceases to be invited to social events that she and her husband once attended. She is no longer recognized as a person in her own right, but becomes the widow *of* such-and-such a person. But she too has difficult personal problems to cope with, particularly if she is an older woman: intense loneliness, little opportunity to meet people, fear of aging, and the disabilities which often accompany it, and feelings of uselessness.

Whatever her status, if she does not or has not had some relationship with a man, preferably marriage, the single woman is seen as a half-person. The young single woman, if she goes to college, is expected to be married by the time she finishes. The divorced woman may need time to consider where her marriage went wrong, but she is expected eventually to remarry. The young widow will *of course* remarry. The older widow may find her fulfillment in her children, but if she is "lucky," she may also find someone and remarry. This is what our family-centered society expects. The questions most often asked of a single woman substantiate these assumptions: "Who's the man in your life these days?" or "When do you think you'll be getting married?" Rarely is the single woman asked what her recent interests are, how her job is going, or what good books she has read lately. A woman is usually seen in terms of her relationship to a man, whether past, present, or future.

Singleness, then, is considered by our "two by two" society as an impermanent, unfulfilled state. With all the emphasis on marriage and family, and all the assumptions about the state of singleness, it is easy to imagine what this does to the frame of mind of the single woman. A young woman may panic at age twenty-two if she is not even close to marriage. The woman who has found an area for expression of her ability and talent through an occupation may feel she is still missing something. The pressures to be married and the assumption that marriage is the only way to live a fulfilled life are so great in our society that even the most alive, whole, growing, single woman may occasionally wonder if she is really getting all that she should out of life.

A friend of mine traveled to her parents' home one Christmas, feeling very good about who she was and where she was as a person. While visiting with her relatives she realized that they were unsure of how to respond to her, she being the only family member present who was single. The relatives could talk to her only about their families; they seemed unable even to ask about her interests. In a subtle way she was excluded from conversations and most of the time she felt that no one could cope with her single, whole, state. Her journey back was filled with sadness because she had not been able to communicate with her relatives, nor they with her. She felt also that somehow she should fit into the same mold as the others and that maybe she did not have it all together after all—maybe she *was* unfulfilled because she had never married. It took her a while to reaffirm herself, her involvements, her interests, and admit that the pervasive societal pressure to get married, as it was expressed through her family, could in fact outweigh her strong self-affirming feelings.

The single woman not only has a great deal to work through in terms of outside pressures; often she also lacks the knowledge of what it takes to survive as a single woman. Many women, especially the widowed or divorced, are finding out the hard way that women are not brought up knowing how to invest well, or take care of a car, or fix a leaky faucet. A deficiency in these skills leaves the divorced or widowed woman, whose husband had always taken care of such things, in a state of helplessness. A woman widowed for several years related to me how good she felt about finally completing an auto maintenance course; she could now protect herself from garage mechanics and car salesmen who take advantage of single women.

The single woman is beginning to choose, and to grow in self-sufficiency. She is beginning to rebel against those negative images. Women who are divorced are choosing not to remarry or deciding to wait until they feel more whole before recommitting themselves. Many younger women are choosing not to rush into marriage until they have a sense of their own personhood—they are loudly and happily affirming singleness. In 1970, 36 percent of all women between the ages of twenty and twenty-four were single compared with 28 percent in 1960. Women *are* discovering new life possibilities.

Living autonomously does not mean living in loneliness. Living as a single woman gives a special privacy, time to experience innermost thoughts, or listen to music, or take a walk, but most important, time to be wholly whatever one is. The fear of being alone is a fear of the unknown. What will I do with myself? Will I get bored with me? If fear can be turned into a spirit of adventure, then living singly opens up all kinds of possibilities for creative exploration in and around the single self. May Sarton, poet and novelist, writes of her experience living a "solitary life":

> Loneliness is most acutely felt with other people. . . . I am lonely only when I am over tired, when I have worked too long without a break, when for the time being I feel empty and need filling up. And I am lonely sometimes when I come back home after a lecture trip, when I have seen a lot of people and talked a lot, and am full to the brim with experience that needs to be sorted out. . . . It takes a while, as I watch the surf blowing up in fountains at the end of the field, but the moment comes when the world falls away, and the self emerges again from the deep unconscious, bringing back all I have recently experienced to be explored and slowly understood, when I can converse again with my own hidden powers, and so grow, and so be renewed, till death do us part.[2]

2. May Sarton, "The Rewards of Living a Solitary Life," *New York Times*, 8 April 1974.

Single women are changing; they are finding the strength to become whole, alive persons. Society's view of them, however, is changing very slowly; there are too many factors blocking a clearer perspective of the single woman as a full person. Among the many hindrances is one that could be of the greatest help—the church. The church has long benefited from the talents and abilities of the single woman but has seldom been supportive in return. It must recognize the single woman as a whole person. It must revise its understanding of "family"—which supposedly means the "family of God" but which, in actuality, has become a structure to meet the needs of nuclear families. Presently, church family dinners, family Christmas programs, and family socials exclude the single woman. A woman I know went to an all-church dinner one night at her new congregation. Arriving in the company of two friends, a married couple, she was promptly escorted to a singles' table set apart from the rest where she was seated with a group of strangers who felt as uncomfortable as she did—*not* the most effective way to go about starting a singles' support group!

The church could be helping young girls to discover many exciting life options in addition to those of wife and mother. Educational materials could show women in the pulpit as minister, girls active in sports, women in various occupations, *as well as* those traditional pictures of little girls working in the kitchen or taking care of baby brother. Women could also be made more visible in the life and activities of the church. If the image of woman can be changed, then the image of the single woman can be changed as well, and she may begin to feel more a part of the church's life. There are other possibilities: counseling, especially for women in transition (widows, divorcées); workshops for women on budget and finance or household and auto repairs; help in job placement; formation of a singles' support group; and, through sermons, dispelling long-held myths about the nature of the single woman.

Obviously the church, like other institutions, needs to open up more of its jobs to single women. It should give them equal consideration in hiring, equal pay, and equal employment practices. For doing the same job today single women get not only less pay than married men but also less pay than single men. Often they are not even hired on the assumption that they will soon get married and leave the job. If they are hired, it will be at a lower salary than a married man would get on the assumption that women have no family to support.

The church could provide strength and support for me if it would begin to affirm my singleness as surely as it affirms marriage, if it were to see me as a full person, with needs different from those of the married couple or family, with my own talents and abilities, my own pain and joy, and my ever-increasing possibilities for becoming whole.

5.

Ambiguous Freedom: Outcries from the Home

LINDA MOYER

In capitalism housework and childcare are lumped together. In fact they are completely different. Housework is drudgery which is best reduced by mechanizing and socializing it, except for cookery, which can be shared. Caring for small children is important and absorbing work, which does not mean that one person should have to do it all the time. But we are taught to think there is something wrong with us if we seek any alternative.[1]

In the variety store where I was shopping recently, I caught sight of a small, familiar-looking woman, a baby hitched up over one shoulder, a toddler by the hand. She looked very competent and matter-of-fact about being there, very *normal*, but the sight of her saddened me inexplicably.

It was not until I was halfway to the car that I remembered who she was. We had known each other several years before when we both were social workers in a public welfare agency. She had come to the agency with a newly-minted master's degree and I remember being very impressed with her skilled analysis and her warmth and concern for her clients. Seeing her years later meandering through the five-and-dime with two young children brought me up short, although the pattern of work-before-house-wife-and-motherhood should not have been surprising to me, since it was also my own.

I tried to analyze my reaction because I realized that I have a set of mostly negative assumptions about a woman with toddlers. First, I assume that she has primary responsibility for the

1. Sheila Rowbotham, *Woman's Consciousness, Man's World* (Baltimore: Penguin Books, 1973), p. 122.

29

care of her children which means, if they are under three at least, that she is never alone. At home she probably does not move from one room to the next without trailing a retinue of children, toys, and blankets; each time she goes out she must first deal with shoes, jackets, diapers, and seat belts. She spends much of her time at home or in the car, doesn't have much time to read, rarely has an uninterrupted conversation. She is probably not employed (although she works nonstop). If she is, it is most likely at a part-time job unsuited to her skills, and to be there at all she must first make elaborate childcare arrangements. I assume that when she does arrange to be away from the children, she must pay a babysitter or be indebted to neighbors or relatives. If the sitter cancels or the children become ill, it is her plans that must change, no one else's. Worse, when she is free of the children she may not know what to do with herself besides shop, as motherhood has forced her interests to dwindle and her network of adult relationships to narrow. In short, I assume she works too hard and has only half a life.

Complaining mothers of young children are frequently admonished that soon they will regard these years as the best of their lives. Those who chide forget that much of the pleasure and satisfaction of the company of young children is dampened by the constant need to protect, provide, and police, and to do housework and shopping with and around them. We are frustrated knowing that although it should be the best time of life, we are often too tired or too busy to enjoy our children. Nor is it true that once the children are in school the job is all over. Should there be a lengthy illness or a teachers' strike the mother must still be home or provide for a replacement.[2]

I suppose, however, that my variety-store friend chose to have children, and that she does not regret it. If pressed, she would probably say, "It's not so bad, I wouldn't have it any other way really." Surely she loves them and wants to be with them as they grow up. Let me stress, lest my own should someday read this, that I do appreciate the oft-listed rewards of

2. For a fuller discussion of the continuous family responsibilities of women see Florence Rush, "Woman in the Middle," *Notes from the Third Year: Women's Liberation*, (New York, New York, 1971), p. 18.

parenthood; I like my children, and delight in their growth, and in no way regret deciding to have them. I do regret, however, that their existence requires, in addition to skirmishes on every front to protect their freedom and safety, a full-scale battle to maintain my functioning, unisolated role in adult society.

Most of the women I know are struggling to find alternatives to doing their own full-time child-care in order to overcome the polarities between the role of housewife and the role of career woman. I refuse the single, though multifaceted, role of cleaner, cook, laundress, nurturant nanny, spiritual glue and kleenex for family. But I equally reject the double role of career mother who works outside the home and administers the family by telephone before and after working hours—not because I don't think children can thrive on good day-care as well as or better than at home with one woman, but because I don't want two full-time jobs.

For those of us who work alone, who need only a typewriter, a potter's wheel, or a sewing machine to ply our trade, the easy answer seems to be to work at home. One types away at that novel while the children are napping, pots while they play in the garden, sews while they watch TV. This is fine for pursuing a hobby, but a serious effort systematically to develop a skill and/or earn money with it is in absolute conflict with high-quality child-care, which demands that one change a diaper when it is soiled, feed a child when she/he is hungry, and not postpone comforting hurt feelings and bumped heads. Creative muses do flee interruptions.

Another apparent option is sharing household respon-sibilities with men. Women who realize that they have been socialized into accepting the burdensome roles assigned to their sex have tried shifting some child-care onto their mates —if they are still around. Willing males range from those who "help" with the children to house-husbands who look after the domestic side while the woman works. There are couples who both go to school or to jobs half-time. In some instances the man still works full-time but pulls his weight after hours and on weekends—not assuming that because he earns the money he is entitled to read the paper and play with the children while she cooks, serves, and cleans up dinner, bathes the kids and puts them to bed, puts away the day's clean laundry, and does a telephoning job for the co-op nursery school.

One might assume, from scanning the above alternatives, that parents need only choose whichever option best applies to them and change accordingly, since it is only reasonable that men should be as responsible for the care of their household and children as women. But privilege is rarely relinquished voluntarily, especially when it is reinforced by the expectations of everyone around that sex role divisions are natural and not to be questioned. And since these notions about "women's work" still prevail in the land, a woman is always one down in her negotiations with even the most enlightened of males. A man totally committed to working away at the most subtle forms of sexism in a relationship still has the full power of the patriarchy behind him should he choose to revert. This built-in inequality in even the most equal of partnerships means that the woman lives in constant tension between her desire to have her needs met and her self-worth affirmed, and her desire to be flexible and supportive in a give-and-take relationship. Insisting too much on the former, she feels selfish and ungiving; should the latter prevail, she may be eaten alive. What to him seems like a generous act, such as caring for the children one extra day in order that she can attend a meeting, may, should she do the same for him, appear like dutiful acquiescence to a preordained state of things—necessary and thus infuriating. She finds herself in an adversary position when she wants to feel like a partner; she ends up feeling grateful when she should feel equal. Resistance from *him* to demands from *her* may make her feel as if the entire relationship is threatened. Women's role has been to maintain the equilibrium in family life; to upset it is to be a "bad wife."

In addition to dealing with the external pressures that make change hard, women must cope with their own inner tendencies toward personal sabotage. We can become convinced that our dissatisfactions and fatigue are due wholly to personal inadequacy, our own inability to cope with the tasks that other women seem to manage effortlessly. We take a dim view of our self-worth and are reluctant to demand our rights. Insecurity about stepping out of a given role is coupled with doubts about whether what we are trying to achieve is worth so much up-heaval. Taught to devalue our work (". . . until I get married," ". . . in case I ever have to support myself") and armed with few positive models for independent achievement at age thirty or forty, we wonder: *what* we can do, and then *if* we can do it, and then again if we really *want* to. It is easier not to rock the boat. Demands that are made with the knowledge that they are only fair and reasonable may, when a woman is alone and has no support for her argument, be reduced in her mind to the shrill and easily-ridiculed sounds of a nagging wife.

My husband (he has a full-time job with somewhat flexible hours and earns most of the money) is responsible for child-care two days out of our six-day work week. He is also responsible for cooking and other household jobs on those days. If a sitter cancels, if a child is sick, I can go on with my plans; I know he is "fathering." Not having my entire life controlled by whims of fate permits me, for a while at least, to regard myself as an independent entity, to take my work seriously, and to be with other adults who nurture it and me. The work progresses, my self-esteem is raised, and I begin to contribute to our income. All these things enable me to return to the family feeling stronger and more able to give of myself.

We did not just decide to change our way of living and then proceed to do so, nor have the changes come about in a smooth and rational way. It has been a volatile process, almost a cycle: crisis—resolution—working on change—semblance of order—crisis. Our questioning of sex roles has forced us to call into question other aspects of our marriage. If we reject traditional "husband" and "wife" roles in certain areas, what else do we reject? How do we make decisions? How do we relate to others? What is the nature of our commitment to each other? The making of changes is a scary process and it is not over yet, but it has helped us to understand each other's fantasies and expectations, and debunk them if necessary, and to see each other in a fresh way while affirming a strong, permanent rela-tionship.

These changes have made several positive differences for our children. Being freed at specified times of the necessity of meeting their physical needs changes my relationship to them. I can be more spontaneous and playful, and a better listener. They now have two people who understand their routines and notions, and in different ways. If one of us is absent for a long while, it is not so upsetting. And the children are receiving positive impressions of adults, both male and female, who assume the multiple roles of family nurture and outside work. This shifting of responsibility also means that my husband has a more direct relationship with the children than he did previously—I no longer have to interpret their unclear speech and moods to him. Just as mothers of newborns learn quickly, out of necessity, how to care for them, fathers rapidly become competent at child-care when they are faced with the necessity of doing it themselves without the convenient buffer of a woman who supposedly can do it better.

Some of our friends laugh at us for being rigid and legalistic, but we find it a relief to know whose turn it is to fix lunch; we don't have to sit back and hope that the other's hunger will drive him/her to the kitchen first. Where chores are not delegated, as in the case of general housecleaning, we each tend to accuse the other of not doing enough.

There are many failings in our system, apart from the obvious one that neither of us can put in a full work week. It is hard to shift the household from one style of operation to another once a week and we have Thursday night "transition tension." I have had to give up control, not to hover over the pots on the stove or linger with the baby. I am often anxious, and sometimes with reason, that the plan might still fail; he will not be able to miss a meeting and I will be left as a loving last resort, at home. (He would no doubt perceive quite different failings!)

I am also aware that this is only a partial and particular solution to the division of labor dilemma. Most men are unable or unwilling to consider such change, either because their jobs are simply not that flexible, or because they are unwilling to exchange voluntarily the public rewards and the concrete, visible struggles of "outside" work for the private and often tedious domestic world. Nor, obviously, does it solve the problems of the single mother, or of the couple who must both work full-time to assure an adequate income.

If our society were a truly humanistic one, that is, if we really loved children, we would all take care of them and give that provision for their care (and for our own—how can we love our children if we do not love ourselves?) top priority. Accordingly, we would provide day-care, excellent schools, and complete medical care. We would place less emphasis on the capital gains from production and more on the well-being of the worker. Therefore we would insist on shorter working hours for everyone, at the same pay, so that parents and others could become involved with children as a matter of pleasure and responsibility, not as a burden. These changes would come about not just to "keep kids off the streets" and make them "productive citizens," or because some cost-benefit analysis indicated that it would be cheaper than crime and welfare, but because we all felt keenly our social responsibility to each other beyond family and class lines, and recognized our common future in our children.

Radical feminist analysis, with which I theoretically agree, finds one of the roots of female oppression in the nuclear family.[3] Even more oppressive is the understanding that it is almost impossible to abandon it. Alternatives to the nuclear family will, if provided by the state in a less than humanistic world, be based inevitably on a model of bureaucratic efficiency rather than on a concern for the well-being of people. Scattered alternative innovations can at best serve only as paradigms for the future; real, permanent change can come only when the alternatives become mass-based and normative. Meanwhile, children continue to be born, and their parents must find ways of working out the feminist dream while struggling with the current reality.

Two people, happily mated, sympathetic physically and mentally, having many common interests and aspirations,

3. See especially Shulamith Firestone, *The Dialectic of Sex* (New York: Bantam Books, 1971).

proceed after marrying to enter upon the business of "keeping house" or "homemaking." This business is not marriage, it is not parentage, it is not child-culture. It is the running of the commissary and dormitory departments of life, with elaborate lavatory processes.[4]

4. Charlotte Perkins Gilman, *The Home* (1903, reprint ed.; Urbana: University of Illinois Press, 1972), p. 69.

PART TWO:

WHAT ARE WE DOING?

6.
We do not want . . .

We do not want
to become like the men
in our society:
  crippled human beings
  under pressure for achieve-
    ment
  emotionally impoverished
  reduced to bureaucrats
  manipulated as specialists
  damned to career-making

We do not want
the sexual privileges and
the sexual stultification of men
genital performance
measured in quantity
sex as merchandise
demanded, bought
paid for and paraded around

We do not want
the nuclear family
divided and dominated by men
existing only for itself
insulating people
making infants of women and
neurotics of adolescents

We do not want
to be provided for—beautified, protected
to feed, train, and adapt our children
to mother and regenerate men

We do not want
to learn what men can do:
to rule and command
to be served, to conquer
to hunt, plunder, and subju-
          gate

—Dorothee Soelle, January 1971
(trans. Erdmut Mueller Brown)

7.

Peace-Working, Women-Working

CAROL NESS and CAROL VALIKAI

Out of an expanding awareness of what it means to work concretely for a peaceful world, we have come to realize that the women's movement and the peace movement are two dimensions of the same struggle. As women working for peace, we are also working to build a new society on an individual as well as an international level, a society in which domination of others and subject/object relationships have no place. In telling you of our involvements in peace work we hope to share also our understanding that a commitment to peace is a natural expression of an integrated life based on wholeness of self and a desire for wholeness for the world in which we live.

We are two women in our mid-twenties, raised in the Lutheran church, who have been drawn into the field of peace work in surprisingly similar ways. Our commitment to peace grew during our college years along with our increasing commitment to Christian values. The institutional church, however, became less of an authority for us as we saw its unwillingness to speak out against social injustice. But, on the edge of the church, and still part of it, was a religious community bringing faith and love together in an active witness against the Viet Nam War and all that is destructive of life. In our specific cases, this was the Lutheran campus ministry at two widely separated state universities. It was a time of rich ferment in that segment of the church, and our theological and political questionings grew side by side, intertwined and supporting one another. As we moved from an "undoubting adolescent faith" to a more life-affirming belief, the old dualisms began to break down.

41

The separations between the sacred and the secular, personal and corporate salvation, and belief and action seemed increasingly false.

The words and stories of the Bible began to take on new meaning. The imagery of the Exodus, moving out from bondage to liberation, gave new significance to current struggles: "next year in the promised land; next year there will be peace in Viet Nam." We saw the Old Testament prophetic witness become a model of faith/action for increasing numbers of clergy and laity who were outraged by the war. The evils that led to and surrounded the war in Indochina were acknowledged as a judgment on a people who were in need of repentance. The lessons of the gospel also deeply affected our thinking about issues of peace and justice. The value which the New Testament places on human life and on peace-making gave new depth and vigor to our own faith, which had formerly been weighted down by an emphasis on otherworldliness and the "fallenness of man."

At the same time, our study and reflection were giving us new insight into the meaning of the Scriptures, and clergy and laity around us were acting on the basis of their scriptural beliefs. They witnessed by marching against the war, counseling draft resistors, and engaging in civil disobedience. Slowly, we began to see this unity of faith and action as a possibility in our own lives.

In addition to our relationship to a concerned community of Christians, other factors contributed to our increasing involvement in peace action. The mood on many campuses in the late sixties was generally one of outrage. We had grown up in the Eisenhower and the Kennedy years and were finally discovering that the United States was not as righteous as we had thought. As we slowly learned of the horrors of the Indochina war, we felt almost a sense of betrayal. When students were shot at Kent State and Jackson State Universities, the sense of shock ran deeper. It was in this frame of mind that we marched, petitioned, and protested to parents, churches, and anyone who would listen. We understood fairly clearly that what our country was doing was wrong; however, we did not understand why it was doing these things.

In the late sixties we saw a country that had made a mistake. We hoped that a movement, through sharing its sense of outrage, could turn America back to its ideals. Since that time we have come to feel that Viet Nam was *not* a mistake (it was government policy) and that the reasons for our nation's involvement in the war and for the repression of the peace movement at home were deeply imbedded in the very nature of American society. We slowly began to realize that protest itself was not enough, but that we needed to commit our lives to long-term organizing if we would build a better world. Many persons in the peace movement were unable to make this transition, and the peace movement as a whole has been criticized for being negative rather than positive in its emphases. Our faith, and the values which had become a part of our very being through our life in the Christian community, helped to sustain us as we reevaluated the nature of the struggle in which we were involved. We realized that the fundamental change that was necessary in our private and corporate lives required full commitment not for a year or two, but for a lifetime.

Because our desire to work for peaceful social change grew out of our faith and an involvement in a Christian community, the "logical" place to begin our work was within the institutional church. We spoke to congregations about the Christian responsibility to work for peace. This was oftentimes a painful experience, especially in the beginning. We still felt very much a part of the Lutheran church, yet it seemed that church members generally, even in our home congregations, separated themselves from us as if we were outsiders. We worked with church-related peace groups such as Clergy and Laity Concerned, and found in them a supportive community for our efforts. While struggling to educate ourselves about the Indochina war, we also worked to raise the consciousness of others. We encouraged them to speak and act through letter-writing, protest, demonstrations, and passing resolutions. When we began, we had little understanding of what working for peace really meant, and acting seemed more important than understanding. Yet, as time went on, we reflected more seriously on the nature of the new society that we were trying to build and the best means for moving in that direction.

Recognizing that peace was not simply an absence of war, but intimately connected with justice and human rights, we came to understand more clearly that we work for peace by working to change society on every level. The interconnections between various issues such as peace and civil rights became more apparent. Our awareness of the inseparability of the peace movement and the women's movement was expanding in several areas simultaneously.

Initially perhaps, our "doing for others" orientation led us easily into the peace movement without challenging our traditional images as women. In a society where a woman's worth is assessed by her ability to be of service to men and children (as wife and mother), it would not be challenging traditional roles to care about the children of Viet Nam. Our work for peace often involved an almost automatic response to the needs of others (Vietnamese refugees, peace movement men) rather than a conscious choice of where to direct our giving. Eventually, however, this orientation required a turning inward to look at ourselves. We began to realize that a commitment to peace is stronger if it grows out of a sense of inner peace and direction. For us this meant finding out more about ourselves as independent and creative human beings, discovering our likes and dislikes, our capabilities, our hopes and fears. Then, in this process of discovery, we came to affirm ourselves as unique, self-determining persons. As we questioned the old ways of operation in areas such as international relations, we began to question them in other areas as well, and to look at society and ourselves in a new way.

During this time of turning inward, as we explored our inner needs and feelings, we developed a growing awareness of our oppression as women and saw this linked to the larger struggle in which we were engaged. Rosemary Ruether, in her book *Liberation Theology*, sees the oppression of women as the oldest form of oppression in human history and as a basic model for all types of social oppression.[1] Understanding the nature of

1. Rosemary Ruether, *Liberation Theology* (New York: Paulist Press, 1972), p. 20.

our own oppression—our inability to be autonomous and self-determining persons—increased our understanding of what oppression means for others. We began to feel that by working to create a world based on peace and justice, we were working to build a better life not only for people "out there" but also for ourselves. By struggling to change our country's military and economic policies, for example, we are working to change a structure that not only affects the lives of many third-world people but also affects us as women in the United States. As long as our country puts such a great emphasis on the military, the needs and concerns of women will not be adequately met. A nation with a strong defense/offense orientation is unfair to women—and to many men as well—because it overemphasizes the traditionally "masculine" methods of solving problems by force, and underemphasizes the more traditionally "feminine" methods of cooperation and reconciliation, and because it does not put a priority on providing for human needs such as day-care and health-care. Slowly, we began to envision what changes must occur if we are to eliminate oppressor/oppressed relationships.

As we became more involved in the women's movement, we saw that by working to bring traditionally "feminine" values, such as compassion and closeness-to-life, into the mainstream of society, we were also working to reduce many of the forces contributing to militarism. We feel that, as women, we need to offer to society a new model for relationships on every level from the personal to the international. A culture based on competition, dominant/subordinate relationships, and lack of reverence for life does not adequately represent the feminine dimension and leads to a militaristic society.

Olive Schreiner, a nineteenth-century author, wrote that war is but a symptom of a crude discoordination of life on earth, a life that is not yet at one with itself. Women and men who see the unity of all life condemn war not only because of its wasteful destruction, but also because it indicates the lack of the coordination, the absence of that harmony which is summed up in the cry, "My little children love one another." The valuing of the masculine over the feminine is another symptom of this discoordination of life. Ms. Schreiner wrote that woman, the bearer of the race, must stand side by side with man, the begetter, if a completed human wisdom, an insight that misses no aspect of human life, is to exist.[2]

The women's movement and the peace movement have a great deal to say to one another about the fundamental changes which must occur if we are to build a world of peace and justice. We feel that if the peace movement is to address itself to the fundamental causes of war, which are rooted in our inability to relate to one another as free and self-determining human beings, then the feminist perspective is absolutely critical. Rosemary Ruether writes:

> We need to build a new co-operative social order out beyond the principle of hierarchy, rule and competitiveness. Starting in the grass roots local units of human society . . . we must create a living pattern of mutuality between men and women, between parents and children, among people in their social, economic and political relationships.[3]

Certainly not everyone in the peace movement would agree that the feminist perspective is essential, so women doing peace work must sometimes struggle with the hierarchy, paternalism, and lack of life-affirming spirit within the peace movement itself as well as within the larger society. We have been involved in peace groups that get bogged down in intellectualizing at the cost of dehumanizing persons. We have felt ourselves caught up in an emphasis on short-term goals and masculine definitions of success that undermines our belief in the value of human life and the need for personal growth. To achieve credibility as women in the peace movement, we have sometimes found ourselves operating under men's rules, vying for leadership, recognition, and status—responding to conditions as they are on other people's terms rather than making conscious choices based on our own values.

2. Olive Schreiner, *A Track to the Water's Edge: The Olive Schreiner Reader*, ed. Howard Thurman (New York: Harper and Row, 1973), pp. 113-14.
3. Ruether, *Liberation Theology*, p. 124.

Working for peace has concrete implications for our day-to-day lives. It means working to reduce our country's militarism by exposing the power of the military/industrial complex. It means changing the ways we relate to the people closest to us and to the larger society as well, in order that all people may be free to make their own choices for their lives. It is a necessity for us, in working for peace, to believe and act as if a peaceful world is possible. Consequently, we work for nuclear disarmament, for cuts in defense spending, and for putting a much higher priority on programs to meet food, housing, and health-care needs. All this demands new thinking about the nature of society and about what we have that we want to protect. We must think about the potential of human beings to base their lives on trust rather than fear, and about the necessity for meeting human needs before peace can be a reality.

It is the way we affirm ourselves that naturally leads to the affirmation of others. This concept contrasts significantly with the commonly-held view that self-denial is the prerequisite for serving other people. Working for the liberation of all peoples is, we believe, not a self-sacrificing act but a self-affirming act. It is incongruous to be for one's self and simultaneously to support systems of oppression. It is equally incongruous to believe that we can be for other people without being for ourselves. Realizing the goodness of the Creator, and that the creation cannot be separated from the Creator, we understand the dignity and worth of all life. Having experienced within ourselves the lowering of the barriers that once prevented our caring for ourselves and for others, we feel that this same experience can be translated corporately. Seeing the hope that is active in our lives, we see also a hope for the world, for when there is hope, there is always a possibility that fear, guilt, and lack of trust can be overcome.

Through the process of being rooted in Christian community, speaking out against the horrors of Viet Nam, and looking deep within ourselves for a commitment to a peaceful world, we discovered a need to make a commitment to our own growth. Affirming ourselves as women and recognizing the need of all persons for liberation suggests a life-style that says no to whatever denies human growth and life. Taking responsibility for our own liberation enables us to be more responsive politically in matters related to prison reform, white racism, and sexism. To be politically responsible in these areas means to see persons as more important than the ideologies we have used to build and defend our elaborate technical systems. Putting ideology first is a death trap. What is needed instead is the steady support and nourishing of that situation, this program, that legislation wherein the primary concern is human need and growth. Such effort emerges out of a vision of the unity of all life. When we see ourselves in relationship to this unity we understand that peace work is integral to what we do and who we are in our daily lives.

8.
Team Ministry as Possibility

BARBARA B. TROXELL

Sunday morning at 9:55 the two clergy, Barbara and George, entered the redwood A-frame building and walked informally down the side aisle of the sanctuary, greeting people along the way. After the prelude, Barbara moved to the center aisle welcoming the congregation to worship. During the service both ministers participated fully, each taking responsibility at different points for prayers, preaching, announcing, and calling the people to be the gathered community. Together they led the celebration of the communion liturgy, assisted by men and women elders. The congregation moved forward to share bread and wine and to offer themselves. "What are your prayers of thanksgiving and intercession?" George asked. The responses came readily —some joyfully, some sorrowfully, some softly, some vigorously. Later Barbara asked, "What are your calls to action?" Announcements were made, help requested, events publicized, new people welcomed. After a benediction, everyone departed for coffee and an adult study hour. Another week in the life of First Presbyterian Church was under way, enhanced by the departing comments of those who once again had celebrated the integrity of worshiping together with a man and a woman sharing full leadership.

As the woman member of this clergy team, I intentionally began this essay with a brief description of that central act of the Christian community, the weekly service of worship. Here we symbolize, dramatize, and rehearse the form and substance of

49

our lives before God. In this context, an important symbolic statement is the presence of a woman and a man leading worship together, each coming to it with his or her own unique experience. The cooperative style, in which both uniqueness and complementarity are affirmed, is essential to a vital team relationship and to a creative way of working within a parish community. Hopefully, the unity-in-diversity manifested in our public leadership of worship on Sunday mornings also continues throughout our daily actions as pastors, administrators, teachers, group leaders, and enablers, functioning within the ministry as a team.

COLLECTIVE MINISTRY OF ALL MEMBERS

Certainly within our parish there are teams and teams and teams. The lay persons of this six-hundred-fifty-member congregation understand themselves to be involved in the decision-making process of the church; they are integral to the parish team. Additionally, six staff persons are employed at First Presbyterian Church: an office manager, a sexton, a half-time music director, a half-time Christian education consultant, and two clergy. This staff functions cooperatively, with strong emphasis in our weekly meetings on participatory decision-making and the recognition of the value of each person's work. The clergy, then, are a team within a team; not isolated, but having particular responsibility for liturgical, pastoral, and administrative leadership within the church.

Historically, women have been solid and strong members of congregations. They have also been employed as office managers, music directors, or Christian education coordinators. But few models exist which show women how to relate cooperatively in pastoral ministry. Through the telling of our stories, those of us involved in woman-man team ministries want to bring to the fore the possibility of such ministry as a viable style within the structures of currently existing local congregations as well as in "specialized ministries." My colleague and I are hopeful that such cooperative ministry may become normative, rather than unusual, in the church.

OUR BACKGROUNDS AND WAYS OF WORK

My experience in professional ministry includes three years as pastor of a small parish on the east coast, followed by seven years as staff person with the student YWCA in two university settings where I worked cooperatively with chaplains and campus ministers. As an ordained person I continued, during those years with the YWCA, to be involved in the enabling of liturgy and the leadership of worship celebrations. In the summer of 1971, I chose to return to parish ministry, maintaining a strong link with campus ministry and higher education, yet eager to be related to a regularly worshiping community of persons of all ages.

The man with whom I share this ministry in a suburban university community is twelve years my senior and has served as pastor of this congregation for seventeen years. He has experienced much growth and many changes in his life. For part of the seventeen years he served as sole pastor; he has also shared the work with four different assistants or associates. Though there is considerable difference in the length of time we have served this church, and though he bears the title "Pastor" while I am "Associate Pastor," we are both committed to seeing our team ministry become ever more creative and fulfilling for the congregation and the community.

The two of us have not divided our pastoral functions in a rigid way. We both enjoy doing liturgy, so we share responsibility for worship leadership. For us, such cooperation is an important sign of the common priestly and prophetic ministry of women and men. Both of us attend meetings of the governing board of the local church, with one of us acting alternately as moderator of the meeting while the other acts as facilitator of the group process. Each of us serves as resource person with several standing committees. We each teach or lead various groups during the course of a year—Bible study, personal reflection, lay planning for Sunday adult study, and confirmation-commissioning classes, as well as groups emerging from the requests and expressed needs of people. I have worked regularly with women's groups in the local church and beyond. He has helped in developing a denominational clergy association, and is related to judicatory committees involved with issues of church and society. These functional divisions of labor, based in part on our diverse interests and skills, are always open for readjustment when we feel another way might be more effective. This spirit of flexibility is a point of strength in our cooperative ministry. When we find ourselves, however, spending too much time working things through, this strength becomes a weakness. Energy, instead of being heightened, is dissipated.

ADVANTAGES AND DISADVANTAGES

The advantages of team ministry are many, but I should like to approach them by first identifying the difficulties and dilemmas we have discovered. First, there are those problems we make for ourselves, when each of us falls into, or traps the other into, patterns which are constricting. There have been times, for example, when I have dumped work on George with an escapist attitude which sounds like, "Well, he's the *pastor!* He's had more experience, and the buck stops with him, so let *him* do it." This obviously plays into the male-superiority stereotype. If he is not conscious of what is happening, he may be flattered—and thereby be trapped—into doing what he really doesn't want to do.

On his part, my colleague has acknowledged that he feels threatened sometimes by my competence and organizing ability. He has found himself feeling, "Women are not supposed to be as competent as men." He says he does not intellectually believe this old stereotype, yet from somewhere in the unconscious the traditional image emerges. So he compliments me for my organizing ability, while at the same time feeling strangely threatened by it.

George is also a man who feels deeply and is utterly open in expressing his vulnerability. At times I have sensed his need for me to be the "strong" one, to help the movement of a worship service or a group process or some other functioning of our team ministry. I have fallen, at such times, into the trap of "parenting" to his "child." *My* deepest feelings are not expressed, for I wonder if there will be anyone to carry the leadership when I am hurting. We have talked very honestly about this concern, and have learned to speak directly to each other when we experience behavior which is not true to our own integrity and not trusting of the other. We have become increasingly aware of our differences, our patterns of behavior, and the psychological traps we set for each other. We are able now, more often than not, to ask the other for help and support. The opportunity for working things through together is one of the great advantages, I have discovered, in a creative ministry.

There are also the problems which come at us from other people, especially those occasions when my status as a minister is called into question. I have been introduced a few times as "the assistant to the pastor," which though unconsciously spoken, is a not-too-subtle form of discrimination. In judicatory meetings some of the male clergy smile paternalistically or become precious about "our woman minister" or simply act as if I were not present. (Other clergymen are learning to call their brothers on sexist statements and actions, rather than always waiting for a woman to raise the issue.) There are also the times when a person not of our parish calls and asks for the pastor, and our secretary indicates that he is not in but that "Ms. Troxell, our associate pastor, is here." There is an audible gasp, or a question about "a *woman* minister?" On it goes. We have found no easy answers in such situations, but there is a real commitment on the part of our whole staff, and on the part of the congregation, to persist in consciousness-raising.

One of the questions raised about shared leadership is whether there are real differences between the ways men and women function in ministry. A strictly affirmative or negative reply does not do justice, it seems to me, to the complexity of the situation. Our differences have developed out of unique life experiences: one of us knows life as a female in this society, the other as a male. Each of us has certain personality traits and patterns that may or may not be directly related to our sexual differences. We do find ourselves reversing the traditional roles in certain instances. For example, my colleague is a man for whom tears come readily and he is not ashamed to let them flow; I am a fairly well-organized woman who likes to see things in logical order. These reversals belie the stereotypes. I would therefore reply to the question in this way: Yes, there are differences emerging from our unique *life* experiences, but the differences are not fixed in relation to our sex differences.

Given this understanding, I have found one advantage of the team ministry to be the opportunity to share our individual insights, born of unique experiences, in the area of theology, biblical studies, liturgy, pastoral care, social concern, group process, and church administration. Through consulting with and challenging each other, we have grown in our understanding of ministry and our ability to relate deeply to persons in crisis. We have discovered, furthermore, that liturgical leadership is fuller with two of us present. We have learned much from each other's observations and feedback after meetings, and have been able together to develop more effective ways of facilitating the process of growth and mission in our church.

The presence of a woman as pastor has meant some new awareness of language in this congregation. Sexist words, I am told, leap out at people in a way they never did before. Though some in the congregation believe the language issue is minor, many of us feel that language both reflects and informs theology, culture, and behavior, and is therefore extremely critical. We wish to be clear in our understanding that God, the Holy One, the Presence at the heart of the world's movement toward wholeness, is not male and should therefore not be spoken of in masculine pronouns. We wish to be clear in our understanding that the gospel is for all people, not simply "all men," whether the term is used generically or not. We have carefully changed words in the printed liturgical orders for Holy Communion and in other prayers in our Worshipbook. We find "people" or "persons" to be fine substitutes for the masculine generic term, and the repetition of the name of God to be quite appropriate in place of the masculine pronouns for the Holy One. Hymn texts still prove problematic, but at least there is awareness. In our preaching and teaching the inclusive terms are used easily by both clergypersons in such a way that it is utterly apparent where our semantic loyalties lie.

A word about the relationship of lay women in the church to ordained women in professional ministry seems appropriate. Though the parish in which I serve has had a long history of strong female leadership among the laity, I am told that my presence as one of the pastors is extremely affirming of this history and continuing work. The contributions of lay women are strengthened by a woman-man team ministry, as all members, women and men, are reminded continually of the possibilities inherent in complementary leadership. It seems important here to mention the image of "servant," so often binding upon women and resented as demeaning of their worth. Yet as Christians we are called, in the words of one of the contemporary creedal statements, to be "servants in the service of God." How can we as women appropriate this image of servanthood and transform it? How can a woman once considered (by others and even by her own self-image) as an inferior, second-class nobody move to being centered in—and committed to the risk-taking inherent in—the Good News of God which involves serving? Perhaps the image of "serving liberator," or "liberating servant," might be more viable, and truer to what women (and men) in the church are called to be.

TEAM MINISTRY AS THEOLOGICAL POSSIBILITY

The greatest value in team ministry may well be the affirmation of wholeness and of liberation to which it points. Our creation, and the essential being of the Creator, were posited in unity. Such is our understanding of Genesis 1:27: So God created persons in his own image; in the image of God he created them; male and female he created them. But the history of humanity has been marked by the sharp fragmenting of this wholeness of God and of creation. The church has not only reflected this brokenness but has too often been one of its initiators. In our day the search and struggle continues for creative unification, in which unique and remarkable differences are not blurred but honored, and offered to the whole. In an incarnational and sacramental perceiving of life and of the world, I believe that a man and a woman standing together in ministry offer an essential symbol of this movement towards creative unification. As brother and sister in the faith, differing in function yet sharing in the life of community with other brothers and sisters, we offer our unique strengths and weaknesses, gifts and graces, convictions and questionings—therein expressing the contrasts and complementarities within the wholeness toward which we are called to move.

But lest "unification" sound too reminiscent of wanting "everything to turn out just right in the end," I would hasten to say that unity without diversity and liberation without struggle are contradictions in terms. Indeed, the polarities of superiority-inferiority, dominance-submission, higher-lower must be broken. Yet these do not die easily. Their death is a threat to all of us, both men and women, for there is security in some of the old hierarchical modes. Yet I believe the effort to free persons from hierarchical sex-role bondage is basic to the living out of the gospel and to the deepest meaning of salvation. And team ministry, worked at creatively by a woman and a man, can be a vital force in this effort.

As we gather round the table to break bread, to share wine, and to offer the prayers of our lives in the community which is First Presbyterian Church, I am reminded again and again of the statement from a letter of our sometimes-difficult brother in the faith, the apostle Paul: "We, many as we are, are one body, for it is one loaf of which we all partake" (1 Cor. 10:17). The loaf is the bread, basic food, staff of life, symbol of transformation. The loaf is also life lived in risk, broken open, offered as possibility for new freedom. In the service of God who calls us to risk justice and love, and in the company of those who seek the vision of wholeness, we, many yet one, move forward to future possibilities of creative ministry.

9.

Reproductive Research and the Image of Woman

KAREN LEBACQZ

Increasing pressure to control the world's population has sparked research in reproductive technology. Such research requires experiments on human subjects, and most of these subjects are women. Already dozens of cases document the abuse of women as experimental subjects in reproductive research. My concern in this chapter is to raise questions about this use of women in reproductive research —questions that probe beyond the research itself to explore the nature, role, and images of women.

Abuse of human subjects in research is certainly not confined to females; however, women may be particularly vulnerable to abuse in reproductive research because of their special role in the reproductive process. A brief look at three experiments which illustrate this vulnerability will not only suggest some procedural safeguards but also open up the larger question of why women are so vulnerable and how this situation and abuse might be mitigated.

Since the Second World War, the Western world has grappled with the question of how to protect human subjects in scientific research. A number of codes have been drafted to ensure adequate protection of experimental subjects from the ambitions of researchers. The first provision of the most famous of these, the Nuremberg code, and of every code that has followed it, is that no research may be done on human subjects without first obtaining the subject's "informed consent." The subject must understand the nature of the experiment, the risks

57

and benefits involved, and must freely consent to participate in it. Observe the following three examples in the light of this principle of informed consent.

Example 1. Research is currently under way to develop techniques for *in vitro* fertilization (fertilization "under glass" in the laboratory).[1] Eggs for this research are being donated by women who are unable to conceive children because the oviducts which normally carry eggs from the ovary to the uterus are blocked. These women donate their eggs in hopes that they may be the recipients of embryos begun *in vitro* and thus have children "of their own." However, the research is in its early developmental stages, and benefits from current experiments will accrue primarily to the researchers and to the scientific community, or possibly to future women, not to these initial research subjects. Yet one researcher is reported to have said, "We tell women with blocked oviducts, 'Your only hope of having a child is to help us. Then maybe we can help you.' "[2] When these women consent to donate their eggs, do they understand that they are not "patients" for whom therapy is forthcoming? Is their consent to the experiment truly informed? Is their desire for children being exploited, even unwittingly, for the benefit of others?

Example 2. If women are vulnerable subjects for research in their desire to *have* children, they are equally vulnerable in their desire *not* to have children. In a recent case in New York, a woman was sterilized by hysterectomy rather than tubal ligation, contrary to the explicit instructions of the hospital director. The doctor in charge justified his choice of the more complicated and dangerous procedure on grounds that surgeons in training needed practice in performing hysterectomies.[3]

The woman had consented to be sterilized. But she had not been informed of the serious nature of hysterectomy or of the

1. See R. G. Edwards and Ruth Fowler, "Human Embryos in the Laboratory," *Scientific American* 223 (December 1970): 44.
2. R. G. Edwards, quoted in *Medical World News*, 4 April 1969, p. 17.
3. Les Payne, "What a Woman Should Know," *San Francisco Chronicle*, 27 February 1974.

availability of a less dangerous alternative. She may have consented to an operation, but her consent can hardly be considered "informed."

Example 3. In an experiment designed to find out whether reported side effects of birth control pills are truly physiological or merely psychological, seventy-six women who came to a Texas clinic seeking contraceptives were given placebo pills. These women were not asked whether they wanted to participate in an experiment or whether they would be willing to risk pregnancy. In flat contradiction to their request for birth control pills, they simply were given placebos.[4]

In the first example cited it is questionable whether the consent given was truly informed. In the second it is clear that the consent given was not informed. And in the third no consent was given at all.

We can see that in all three examples the benefits from the research are directed not toward the participating women, but toward other parties. Research in *in vitro* fertilization promises a number of rewards to the scientific community: fundamental knowledge about embryonic development, the possible development of new methods of contraception, and of course the notoriety that will come to the first researcher who successfully produces a "test tube" baby. In the hysterectomy case, the benefits went to the young surgeons who gained medical experience. The experiment on oral contraceptives produced knowledge about effects of the Pill. The justification for the experiments in all three cases, therefore, lies in the benefits of increased knowledge that accrue to the scientific community or to the public at large. The researchers appear to have rationalized the risks involved on the grounds of a "greater" good to be created.

At stake here is a primary question of *loyalties*. In all three cases, those who were responsible for the well-being of the women involved demonstrated that their primary loyalty was not to these women, but to some other party. On that basis they

4. See Robert M. Veatch, "Experimental Pregnancy," *Hastings Center Report* 1, no. 1 (June 1971).

were willing to violate established rules for research. In the language of ethics, we would say that they used a "utilitarian" mode of reasoning to justify their actions, that is, "the greatest good for the greatest number." But it was precisely to counter-balance this kind of reasoning that the principle of informed consent was established, so that human subjects do not become "guinea pigs" for the benefit of others.

In the three examples cited the question of loyalties is par-ticularly troubling because the women involved were not sim-ply research subjects but also patients. It is understandable that a laboratory researcher is interested in the accumulation of scientific knowledge and gives primary loyalty to scientific concerns. In contrast, the physician is expected to give primary loyalty to the needs and well-being of the patient. This primary loyalty undergirds the relationship of trust between physician and patient; its violation strikes at the heart of medical practice. All of the women mentioned were seeking medical interven-tion for a specific concern; they were entitled therefore to the primary loyalty of their physicians.

In view of the violation of the principle of informed consent and of the misdirection of the loyalties of medical practitioners as demonstrated in these three examples, I suggest that pro-cedural safeguards need to be established to protect women in reproductive research. The first such safeguard is the creation of an "advocate" whose primary loyalty is to the individual woman and who will promote her interests and well-being over against the interests of the general public or the scientific community. Such an advocate would make sure that the principle of informed consent is not violated by ambitious researchers.

In addition to the violation of informed consent, other trou-bling aspects of these experiments demand further safeguards. In the second and third examples cited, the women involved were poor, multiparous (having given birth to two or more children), nonwhite women. Exploitation of the poor and of minority group persons is a particularly ominous aspect of the misuse of human subjects in experimentation. Many of these women were also in jeopardy because of language or cultural gaps. Their protection against abuse in research therefore requires a special kind of advocacy. Further, in their desire to avoid pregnancy, women are not only vulnerable, they are profitable. The experiment on contraceptives was funded by a manufacturer of oral contraceptives. In the first two years after this company put its first oral contraceptive on the market, sales jumped an astounding $30 million, yielding a net increase in earnings of $10.5 million.[5] The potential profit motive of corporations makes it imperative that consent not be considered "informed" unless the subject understands that the research is being sponsored by a company with a vested interest in the outcome.

The contraceptive experiment is particularly troubling also because it resulted in ten pregnancies—pregnancies in women who had sought medical help precisely to avoid pregnancy! When inquiries were made as to the responsibility taken by the researcher for these unwanted pregnancies, he is reported to have said that he would have aborted them if the Texas statutes "weren't in limbo right now."[6] Apparently no other provision was made to compensate these women for this possible result of the experiment. Indeed, it has been remarked that experiments resulting in unwanted pregnancy are so frequent that it should be a matter of policy for the sponsoring agency to be clearly obligated for such possible results. Moreover, the response of this researcher—his claim that he "could have aborted them"—ignores the fact that most of these women were Mexican-American women for whom abortion might not have been an option because of their religious beliefs. To impose a "remedy" acceptable to middle-class Americans onto other groups of persons raises serious questions about definitions of normative life-styles and class status and the way woman, herself, is defined.

Beyond the questions about the nature of informed consent and the structure of experiments involving women as research subjects there is the larger question: Why are women so vulnerable to abuse in reproductive research?

---

5. From the Annual Reports of Syntex Labs, summarized in Reinier Lock, "Profit and the Pill," (unpub. ms., Boalt Hall, University of California, Berkeley, June 1971).
6. Veatch, "Experimental Pregnancy," p. 3.

A partial answer to this question lies in the desires of women to have or to not have children. Our desires make us vulnerable. They may be based on role expectations, or on societal images of "the good life" for women. Thus, the vulnerability of the women in the first example derives in part from their desire to fulfill what has traditionally been expected of women: the bearing of children "of their own." In the second and third examples the women may have been particularly defenseless because of language or cultural barriers, but they represent the position of *all* women who for social, economic, or personal reasons desire medical intervention to prevent conception.

The abuse of women in reproductive research, therefore, must be seen not only as a matter of unethical practice on the part of researchers or faulty structuring of experimental design. It is also, and fundamentally, a question of women's roles and images in society. If women are coerced into particular roles or have only limited modes of expression available, they become especially vulnerable to what I call the "magic bullets" approach to reproduction. In this approach, a norm for reproduction is established—e.g., "children of your own," or "no more than two children"—and deviations from the norm are defined as "bad" or "irresponsible." Then magic bullets are sought to eradicate such deviations. Technologies such as *in vitro* fertilization or the Pill emerge, promising such great rewards in eradicating "abnormalities" that any cost is considered worth the benefits to be gained. The ends come to justify the means, and the rights of women are jeopardized for "the greater good of the greater number." Therefore, we must pay attention to the symbols and presuppositions which define the "good life" for women, for it is these which foster the abuse of research subjects.

At this time in our history, pressures are building to reduce population size. Traditional role expectations that require women to bear children are being replaced by new expectations that require women to limit the number of children they bear. Women are increasingly expected to seek contraceptive help. This suggests that we must be particularly wary of the "magic bullets" approach in which techniques of contraception are foisted on women in research without due protection. One physician has suggested that the mass consumption of the Pill constitutes "one of the largest mass human experiments . . . ever considered."[7] An estimated twenty-five million women may be participating in this experiment without even realizing that they are experimental subjects, human "guinea pigs."

Particular care must be taken not to impose a majority conception of the "good life" on the women of minority groups. We have cited above the callousness of one researcher who would have imposed his middle-class "solution" on a problem for which he was responsible. Women from minority groups may already be in a position of special vulnerability vis-à-vis medical research. This would also be heightened by the efforts of others to make them conform to a norm of childbearing in a "magic bullets" approach. One black woman gives poignant articulation to this danger:

> The worst of it is that they try to get you to plan your kids by the year; except they mean by the ten year plan, one every ten years. The truth is, they don't want you to have any, if they could help it. . . . Even without children my life would still be bad—they're not going to give us what *they* have, the birth control people. They just want us to be a poor version of them only without óur children. . . .[8]

The "good life" for women must be understood to mean more than simply conception control. It must also include freedom, and protection from coercion in all its forms—freedom from the imposition of role expectations that create desires which, in turn, foster reproductive vulnerability. The abuse of women in research is a serious matter demanding investigation. But beyond and beneath the research lies the more fundamental and ultimately critical question of woman's image.

7. Francis D. Moore, "Ethical Boundaries in Initial Clinical Trials," in *Experimentation with Human Subjects*, ed. Paul A. Freund (New York: George Braziller, 1969), p. 363.
8. From Robert Coles, *Children of Crisis*, quoted by Arthur J. Dyck, "Procreative Rights and Population Policy," *Hastings Center Studies* 1, no. 1 (1973): 75.

10

Daring to Grow

PAT DRISCOLL

It's great to be a woman today. I, a Christian feminist with a grand husband, fine family, and a personal involvement in lay theology, am happier than I ever thought I would be at age forty-nine. Our large family—eleven children—has meant work and problems as well as joys. However, the roles of wife and mother, rather than thwarting my personhood or stunting my artistic growth, have enriched me. My activities in civic, political, school, church, and fraternal affairs have given me experience and confidence in writing, speaking, and organizing.

A sense of purpose contributes to my fulfillment. For twenty years I have been developing a fresh focus on Mary, Mother of Jesus, as woman-with-child, our universal mother and symbol of ecumenical unity and feminist solidarity. Although I thought I understood Our Lady before, only now does she emerge as a loving, supportive mother and sister. I see her shedding her religious "madonna" image and living among us as warmly wonderful *Woman of New Life*. She is the *New Woman* we all dream of becoming: caring, joyful, free, creative, and totally fulfilled. In unique ways all of us are given a share in Mary's *Theotokos* (God-bearing) honor—valid role model for all.

My interest in lay theology began when I was expecting my fourth child. I wanted to relate to Mary, once pregnant with Jesus. The universal symbolism of pregnancy as promise of new life, growth, and rebirth took hold of my imagination. First, I sought to express through sketches and statues her prebirth period. In between home duties I researched the theme in art and found a few definitely expectant Marys (a bas-relief in Notre Dame Cathedral, Paris, and an Italian painting,

"Madonna del Parto" by Piero Della Francesca). I felt pregnant
with the Marian cause—as though I were a part of the very
image on which I was working. A sense of dignity, gratitude,
and responsiveness nourished me.
My concern for specialized devotion for mothers-to-be led to
consultations with artists, publishers, and clergymen. I composed the following prayer which I originally entitled "A
Prayer to Our Lady of Pregnancy." Church authorities, while
admitting the doctrinal truths and historical precedents involved, refused official approval "on the grounds of indelicacy"
for years. I was angry and frustrated. Mary's pregnancy wasn't
my invention but God's chosen way of bringing Jesus Christ to
us. However, when I changed the title to "Our Lady of Maternity" the Bishop of Oakland granted the *imprimatur:*

> *O Mary,*
> *Pregnant with the Word-Made-Flesh,*
> *Pray for us, your daughters,*
> *And for our unborn children.*
>
> *Help us who have conceived*
> *To wait in patience,*
> *Labor in love,*
> *And deliver in joy.*
>
> *Grant that all who labor in this life*
> *May find deliverance from evil*
> *And rebirth into everlasting joy*
> *Through the Blessed Fruit of Thy Womb,*
> *Jesus!*
>
> *Holy Mary, Mother of God,*
> *Pray for us now*
> *And at the hour of our delivery. Amen*

My efforts, originally home-bound, led to contacts with international figures. On a trip to Europe I was able to meet with
several theologians whom I knew had special interest in the
role of Mary. I received some encouragement from Protestant
monk Max Thurian of Taizé in France, author of respected
papers on the Blessed Virgin. The Reverend Eric Mascall, an

Anglican theologian of Kings College in London, was also helpful. Through him I joined the Ecumenical Society of The Blessed Virgin Mary. The late Michael Cardinal Browne of the Vatican agreed to advance the pregnant madonna's cause in Rome. The private audience with Cardinal Browne enhanced my apostolate. "It is a lovely devotion for young mothers, Mrs. Driscoll," the venerable prelate said, "but of what possible significance for the ordinary Christian?"

"She is the symbol and identity we all need, Your Eminence," I replied, "because women and men alike, as members of the Church on earth, are laboring to bring forth Christ." "Also," I emphasized, "Mary is still pregnant spiritually with each one of us, who is part of the whole Christ, until our rebirth into eternal life."

"Your theology is very sound," he smiled. But six months later, the Cardinal's letter brought the disappointing news that the Vatican response had been negative.

Prior to 1969, the historic year of humankind's first walk on the moon, I had prophetically sculptured a small plaque of Mary, pregnant and standing on the moon. This image is found in St. John's Apocalypse: "And a great portent appeared in heaven, a woman clothed with the sun, with the moon under her feet, and on her head a crown of twelve stars; she was with child and she cried out in her pangs of birth, in anguish for delivery" (Rev. 12:1, 2). I felt so strongly about this that the following year when I was in Houston, Texas (home of NASA, the Space Center), I presented a madonna of the space age to Lee Kerwin, wife of Astronaut Dr. Joseph Kerwin, as symbol of Mary's relevance to our space-age generation which her husband helped launch. I continued my work on Mary. Interest in the pregnant madonna grew.

There are heartaches in this self-appointed apostolate of a life-affirming madonna: sneers, being regarded as a fool or a religious nut, occasionally feeling all alone, and even antagonism. One year I was saddened when the little ceramic mother-to-be, which my pastor had requested, disappeared from the center of the advent wreath in our church. But in a larger perspective these are trivia. Mary *is* pregnant with promise and a new birth is inevitable.

The youth rebellion, the fall-out from Vatican II, and the upsurge of feminism had begun to unsettle suburbia. Mothers, hearing the assurances from the women's liberation movement that we would have to leave our homes in order to grow, were alarmed; and the pulpit, which had served as a haven of security for many of us, tossed out no lifeline to save us from our floundering. My assumptions about the rewards of traditional family life were challenged from all directions. Fortunately there was another mother who shared my distress and also shared my vision of what the pregnant Mary might bring to women, the church, and the world. We felt the need of a living symbol of promise and hope, growth and rebirth. We worked through our own crisis of identity, direction, and fulfillment by coauthoring and teaching a series of womanhood courses in which we affirm Christian values in this time of confusion.

Because "womanhood" sounded archaic we coined the word "womanity" (woman integrated with humanity). We applaud the women's movement for challenging women and men to confront the injustices and influences which stunt growth toward full personhood. We reject, however, those ideas which are destructive of life on any level. We distinguish our perspective from the secular one. Christian Womanity is feminism committed to Christ, our Liberator; appreciative of Mary, the ideal feminist; dedicated to life on all levels (physical, emotional, spiritual); and working toward mature personhood. Women of all ages have participated in our studies and small group discussions. Knowledge about our work is spreading to other states and to England, and our programs are catalogued in the foremost Marian library in Dayton, Ohio.

Something is forming through Mary for us: a sense of the unity of the secular and spiritual identity of the *New Woman.* Pope Paul affirms this in his 1974 exhortation on Mary, "Marialis Cultus," looking on her as the *New Woman* and perfect Christian.

Mary's advice at the marriage feast of Cana, "Do whatever He tells you," guides me. In accepting, as did Mary, total dependence on my Creator, I become open in faith to his Spirit. I am "filling the water jars," trying to do my best in the projects I undertake, enjoying my work—confident that her son, Jesus, will change my water into his wine at the right time. Trusting him releases all my energies. I feel launched from my ego-pad and soaring into the future. Now everything has value.

In daring thus to promote the Blessed Virgin's relevant role, I am growing. There is a definite rhythm in my work: prayer, solitude, and contemplation are the still periods in between my laboring. Then purposefully, like contractions all working toward some glorious birth, comes action: designing, writing, lecturing, sculpturing, attending conferences.

Christian Womanity offers an identity to Christian women. We do not now see it as an activist movement. With a unifying vision of ourselves as *New Women* or *Women of New Life*, we personify the Church on earth mystically pregnant with Christ and in labor to bring him forth. As in the apocalyptic vision we see woman clothed in the "Sun of God" and crowned with the twelve values of Christian Womanity (appreciation, awareness, acceptance, action, attitude, joy, generosity, faith, compassion, courage, hope, and love). The moon under her feet reminds us that we have entered the space age. If we accept our life-nourishing dignity, we can grow where we are planted and bear fruit in loving service.

11.

WE, as Ministers, AMEN!

KAREN L. BLOOMQUIST

I, Karen, am a minister, and I am becoming *more* of a minister! This is an affirmation I continually have had to make as a woman preparing for ordination in the American Lutheran Church. Weighted down by a tradition biased against woman's affirmation of self, the "official" church and seminary have tended to negate such an affirmation on my part. The negation is expressed very subtly: "Do you *really* want to become an ordained parish minister?" or "Oh, yes, this person is well qualified for the ministry, but what local congregation would ever consider calling a *woman!*" That's where the lack of acceptance lies, they say, on the parish level. Yet I experience more genuine acceptance from the persons to whom and with whom I minister, that is, those on the local level. Within that context I can boldly proclaim, "I am minister!" It seems to me that the "official" church is afraid to affirm what the "grass roots" level has known all along: that women are ministers, and have been the embodiments of the "ministerial qualities" in our culture for a long, long time.

It might seem that my pursuit of ordination is a radical departure from the traditional role of women in the church. But rather than separate myself from what women's roles have been, I choose to see my ministry in continuity with them. In the home, women have nurtured the family and attended to the total needs of all its members. Often we have even sacrificed our own lives for the sake of husband and children. The church has recognized, even sanctified, the crucial role of women in caring for the family, but without acknowledging that this same nurturing servant role is basic to most conceptions of the role of the

69

ordained minister (who cares for his/her "flock"). Women have
also tended to be the religious teachers in the home, and later in
church schools. When the church became instrumental in es-
tablishing the "caring" vocations as extensions of its ministry
into the wider community, these positions were filled largely
by women. The present-day vocations of social work, nursing,
and the teaching of small children are similarly filled today.

The model of the ideal Christian life, that of self-sacrificing
love for others, has been tragically emulated by women. We
have probably lived up to that ideal more than the pedestaled
male clergy. The theme has been so pervasive in our lives that
when our services have been employed by the church, it has
usually meant no pay or, at best, a minimal wage. (Note the
thousands of hours of volunteer church labor by women, and
the low wages of most church secretaries.) This is a trap that
ordained women must not fall into.

In the one arena where women have taken active leadership
roles, the women's organization, they have not been taken
seriously by the rest of the church, and especially by the clergy.
When women's auxiliary participation in the church became
institutionalized in the late nineteenth century, there seemed
to be little thought for what this separate sphere of "women's
work" would mean in the total life of the church. Seldom has
the ministry of the women's organization been referred to as
the ministry of the church. Women do more than their share of
the church's work, usually without any recognized authority.

In the early church there is evidence that women did have
active, recognized ministries. Yet in recent centuries, women's
roles, in almost all cases, have been confined to that of a serving
relationship to Christ and to the male leaders of the church.
Woman has been seen as "Other," as derivatively defined in
relation to man, the standard, the authority, the initiator, and
the definer of her ministry. In denominations where women
have been ordained, those who serve a parish usually have a
subordinate position in relationship to a male pastor, or are
called to a parish unable to secure a male pastor.

Further, women clergy are often set off as a separate caste,
distinct from the rest of the churchwomen, and identified with

the male clergy. I don't want that to happen to me; as a clergy-woman, I feel my potential for facilitating and affirming the ministry of *all* persons in the church, women and men alike. However, if all women are to be affirmed, there must first be a neutralizing of the resistance felt by women generally toward women in leadership positions. The reasons for this resistance are many and varied. Some women feel that their traditional roles and the inherent maleness of the clergy are God-ordained. Others feel trapped in their present roles and are envious of women who break out of nontraditional patterns. Some regret having given up their career for a family, and they resent other women who do not do likewise. Others simply feel threatened by any change affecting them. But the overarching reason for resistance seems to be the pervasively negative self-image that we as women are conditioned to have.

My pursuit of ordination has not been without ambivalence. Some within the women's movement insist that ordination indicates "giving in" to the male-determined authority struc-ture of the church. I also realize that it tends to set some women above others—a contradiction of the nonhierarchical sister-hood emerging today. These considerations, along with the oppression and pain of exclusion that I have experienced in seminary, could have led to an abandonment of my ordination goal. But through it all, my sense of call has intensified—a call to help bring renewal and life to persons (and structures) so that they might more fully realize their humanity. It is important for me to gain a foothold in the clerical leadership of the church, which sorely needs to utilize the perspectives of both sexes. It is important for me as an ordained person to symbolize and thus "call forth" the authority that all women have within them-selves for ministry, whatever their position or vocation. Poten-tially, ordination of women can serve as a symbol and motivat-ing power for other women and men to claim their own minis-tries rather than unquestioningly accepting a derivative status in the church. The lay ministry of the church needs to be affirmed in its own right, rather than treated as secondary to that of the ordained.

I see ordination as a kind of delegation of authority by the

church. It is often emphasized in Protestant circles that the
Word of God is the ordinand's sole authority, that she/he is set
apart from the laity in function only. But it is through the person
that the authority is embodied, that the Word of God is brought
to life in the present. I am empowered by God *through* the
community to act and speak on behalf of it. The channel of
authority should be horizontal rather than vertical. Ordination
does not grant me dominion over others, because true authority
negates the inequality implied in the phrase "dominion *over.*"
Authority as embodied by Moses and Deborah and Jesus involved an identification *with* the people, and through that
identification, the welling up of divine love and power. It
involves the calling forth of the deepest expressions of the
other person.

As women today begin to identify more fully with each other,
spokeswomen with this true authority are rising from within
and on behalf of the community. In the past, women's negative
self-images—and hence dislike of other women—have in part
deterred the emergence of female embodiments of authority. If
we are to possess power, and be able to delegate it to other
women, we must *like* ourselves and have positive self-images.
Ordained women who have been authorized through the community of women and men are necessarily enmeshed in this
process. To exercise the authority that comes to me through
ordination I must call forth all that I am and all that others
(especially other women) are or can be. As ordained pastor, I
should be challenging others to take hold of the authority given
them in baptism.

I am called by the community to administer the sacraments,
those earthly channels of divine grace. While the sacraments,
rightly administered, proclaim and thus embody the promise of
God, this grace cannot be restricted to the officially recognized
sacraments. All of creation is sacramental. The water, bread,
and wine bear God's presence to the faithful, but likewise all of
creation, including God's people, bears God's presence. Why
not extend the consecration of the communion elements (a
crucial role of the ordained office) to include also the sacramental "consecration" of persons? Is that not what the real ministry

of the church is about? That is also what women (and laymen) have lacked in their "unofficial" ministries in the church—a full authorization of the ministry of their very person.

I take for the model of my sacramental ministry the actions and words of Jesus at his Last Supper: He (1) took bread, (2) and when he had given thanks (3) he broke it and gave it to them, (4) saying, "This is my body" (Luke 22:19). In keeping with the theme that the ordained ministry of women has the potential for calling forth and empowering others, I choose to focus on the sacramental "consecration" of women, recognizing that the actions involved apply to women and men alike.

1) "Taking" involves an action, an action which calls attention to something. In the Eucharist this "taking" action most commonly involves a "raising up" or "holding forth." Women have traditionally not been involved in raising up or holding forth their own lives. Instead of naming ourselves we have let others name us. Our lives have been held up and named usually in terms of our relation—or lack of relation—to a male. In common practice the husband's first name actually becomes a new first name for the wife. The woman is "held up" as Mrs. John Doe. She is known, and knows herself, primarily in her relatedness to husband and children. If she is left without them she finds herself bereft of an identity and without a life of her own.

To take hold of my life is to name the stuff of my life. It is to show forth what it is that makes me who I am, and to encourage others to do the same. We hold up our life stories, our autobiographies, with all their gaps, embarrassments, lost dreams, and pains. We make the common and ordinary, distinctive and special. It is the first stage of the sacramental act—the taking of bread and of all that has gone into making it bread. It is the raising up of the cup of wine, of that which washes away the coarseness of the dry crumbs and the brokenness of our lives. The bread and wine are symbols of the stuff of life; the pains, joys, and ordinariness are mingled and raised up together.

2) The naming and raising up of who we are as women leads to the second stage of the sacramental act, the *affirming* of where we are, who we are, and of where or how we are moving.

It is in naming the stuff of our lives that we begin to think about what we have to affirm. Affirmation thus becomes a giving of thanks for who we are, an act that can best occur in community rather than in private—not in a "mutual admiration society" but in a genuine community which accepts the personhood of each member. The emergence of personhood is encouraged where it seemed lacking before. This giving of thanks becomes a celebration of the diversity that each brings to the whole, and thereby a discovery of commonality. Affirmation is the blessing, the "thanks-giving" of the sacramental act—a thanksgiving for each other.

Many women have been unable maturely to affirm themselves in this way. Once we have "held up our lives" the negativities have often loomed too large and painful to overcome. We become envious and sometimes feel threatened by those women who are able to affirm themselves and act on the basis of that affirmation.

3) The *breaking* "of bread" is the action most common to women. This is where we have traditionally inserted ourselves into the sacramental activity. The self-sacrificing, breaking, and giving of ourselves has been no problem for us. The real problem is that we are so used to giving of ourselves that we've omitted the first two stages of the sacramental act. Unless we have something to name or take hold of, something to affirm, what is there left to break in self-giving love? Women have given of themselves for many a worthy cause both within and outside the church. The giving that involves one's self, not just one's possessions, is the real "breaking of bread" for one's sisters and brothers. Because woman's giving of self has often been done in a volunteer context, the essential nature of giving has been preserved. In contrast, it has often been distorted in the male-dominated arena of price-tagged labor for self-interest.

But it should be a positive, whole self which is broken, not a segment of a self, not one defined primarily through another, not one pervaded with a negative self-image. Only when I can first affirm myself will I really be able to give something in the breaking—break a whole in such a way that others may receive something! Only a gift that has been lifted up and affirmed, that has self-acknowledged worth and value, is able to nourish and sustain others, and inspire them to engage in the sacramental process of life.

4) The bold proclamation of the words is the fourth and crucial aspect of the sacramental activity ("saying, 'This is my body' "). Women are not used to being speakers. Our words have usually not been heard, and when we have spoken it has usually been in private spheres, or else through a male. This has been especially true in the church. When women have broken and shared their lives in isolation from the holding up and affirming of their lives, the words have also been spoken by others for them: "Let the women *make* the blankets and the food, and *do* the other sundry tasks on behalf of the church; the men will *speak* for and to the church." Thus, the split between women's actions and words has been perpetuated.

But the silence is breaking. Women are beginning to speak with new voices rising out of their experience. What has been held up and affirmed is being broken and shared in living. What has occurred now begs to be proclaimed. If something of women's lives has been broken and shared, then something of women's words needs also to be shared. We are beginning to *own* through our words what we have been and are becoming in the church. In doing so, we experience a new-found solidarity with one another. The words are spoken from the context of, and contribute toward, a realization of "the Body of Christ" as a corporate reality.

When women have been given authority in the church, the one activity most consistently held back from them has been that of presiding over the Eucharist, the highpoint of the church's life. As long as women are absent as celebrants of this sacrament, no matter how fully they are included in the rest of the church's ministry, the church will continue to represent unwholeness for women; and the subservience of women to men in other arenas of life will continue to be sanctified.

As a woman entering the ministry, its sacramental aspect, in the wider sense described above, is crucial to me. I am called to "consecrate the elements"—the people—through whom we know God's presence and grace. Such a call necessitates identification *with* other people, especially other women, not separation from them. For it is within the bonds of the "Body" that I receive the real authorization of my ministry. At that point, the affirmation no longer is "I am minister." It becomes instead a common affirmation of "WE as ministers, AMEN!"

PART THREE:

WHERE ARE WE GOING?

12.

Meditation on Luke 1:46-55 (NEB)

It is written that Mary said:
Tell out, my soul, the greatness of the Lord,
rejoice, rejoice, my spirit, in God my saviour;
so tenderly has he looked upon his servant,
* humble as she is.*
For, from this day forth,
all generations will count me blessed....

today we shall say:
  my soul sees the land of freedom and
  my spirit will deliver itself from fear,
  the empty faces of women
    will be filled with life and
  we will become human beings—
  awaited by generations before us
    who were sacrificed;

It is written that Mary said:
so wonderfully has he dealt with me,
* the Lord, the Mighty One.*
* His name is Holy;*
his mercy sure from generation to generation....

today we shall say:
  the great transformation which is happening
    in us and through us
  will happen in everyone, or
    not happen at all
  there will be mercy
    when the dependent can abandon the wasted life and
    learn to live themselves;

It is written that Mary said:
  the deeds his own right arm has done
  disclose his might:
  the arrogant of heart and mind he has put to rout,
  he has brought down monarchs from their thrones,
  but the humble have been lifted high. . . .

today we shall say:
  we will disown those who own us and
  we will respond with laughter
    to those who know the nature of woman;
  the rule of males over females will come to an end—
    objects will become subjects who
    win their own and better right;

It is written that Mary said:
  the hungry he has satisfied with good things,
    the rich sent empty away.
  He has ranged himself at the side of Israel his servant; . . .
  he has not forgotten to show mercy. . . .

today we shall say:
  women will travel to the moon and
  women will make decisions in the parliaments
  their desires for self determination
    will come to fulfillment and
  emptiness will be upon those greedy for power—
    their fears will become immaterial and
    the exploitation will come to an end.

                              —Dorothee Soelle, January 1971
                              (trans. Erdmut Mueller Brown)

13.

The Emancipation That Never Happened

DOROTHEE SOELLE

"The freedom, children, it never came."
—Bertold Brecht, 1927

The women's movement, so I am told, has reached its goals. The slave and servant of man has become his independent partner, equal to him in status and legal rights. Whereas a Gallic synod, held in Macon in the sixth century, could still raise the question whether a woman was to be considered a human being, many employers in the twentieth century have *even* gone so far (supposedly) as to pay equal wages for equal work. The barriers of the notorious three Ks—*Kinder, Küche, und Kirche* (children, kitchen, and church)—have allegedly been broken down. I am assured that the possibilities for vocational achievement are the same for men and women, and that the social prestige of unmarried working women is slowly rising. The emancipation of women has been a *fait accompli* for a long time, so I am told.

As of yet, I have been unable to find convincing evidence of this supposedly obvious fact. On the contrary, many indicators lead me to believe that the voice of women is completely ignored in public affairs in my country, from the educational system to urban development. As far as the legal status of women is concerned, I discover that what may be right for the married woman is by no means self-evident or sanctioned for the unmarried mother. Vocational possibilities for men and women are equal only as regards low-level and at best middle-level positions. A young woman who wishes to participate in a master's training program at a factory finds herself confronted

81

with such difficulties, even before she gets a chance to prove herself, that she prefers to give up at the outset. The taboos of society are firmly entrenched: "I will never let a woman order me around!" Women become weary when they continually come up against such a wall of prejudice. They are no longer interested in fighting for better positions and greater responsibilities, and this only reinforces the patriarchal opinion of the male overlords: "We would have liked to hire a woman, but women don't want to do this." The result is a vicious circle: Prejudice on the part of a society causes resignation on the part of women, and this in turn brings about an even more deeply engrained prejudice which considers itself vindicated by experience.

What has really been done so far to further the cause of emancipation? Well, women have acquired some rights, for example, the right to an education or, to put it more modestly, the right to pursue a course of training. Yet some 60 percent of the parents in the Federal Republic of Germany still think, "She's only a girl, she doesn't need to learn anything." True, we have gained the right to the free exercise of a profession. At the same time, however, that profession loses stature in the eyes of the public the moment it comes to be considered "woman's work." The result is no possibilities for advancement, only a moderate salary, and incredibly low social prestige. It seems to me that, if anything, the stultification of women is on the increase.

The reason for this state of affairs we are always told is the "nature of woman." Men have of course known all about woman's "nature" since time began. They have labeled certain human characteristics "feminine," packaged and promoted these characteristics as convenient and advantageous for society. "Just like a woman!" they say, even in serious discussion, and I know exactly what is meant: nice, and imaginative, but irrational, impossible to argue with. Thus woman's "nature" has been all wrapped up in a neat little package. But it could be that for woman herself this "nature" has not yet been finally fixed. It could be that her own search for identity in a changed world has just begun. At this time we hardly know what will happen to the "nature of woman" if she no longer bears twelve children but only two. Our country is still dominated largely by the view that marriage is what makes the life of a woman. The years which precede marriage, the years of education and professional activity, are considered purely preparatory for the real thing—marriage. This model, to which single women continue to conform, confirms my suspicion that emancipation has not yet taken place in Germany.

But what does the term emancipation actually mean to us? What kind of liberation are we thinking of? What sort of freedom are we talking about? Is it the freedom to share in a piece of the cake? Do we mean that women should be content to reach the same levels as men, that they should be allowed to think and do everything that men alone had been privileged to think and do up until now? Do women in their vision of emancipation see nothing beyond the horizons they already know from experience? Do we women want something only for ourselves, or do we, in and through our personal desires, seek something for the world in which we live as well? Is the issue at stake the big "Me Too," or is it a larger "Other"?

Emancipation, including that of young people, of workers, and of black people, always remains too restricted in its focus if it seeks to gain only that which others already "have" and we do not yet "have." Emancipation does not mean the accommodation of women to a world that is fashioned and administered, or in any case determined, by men. True emancipation is not interested in simply parroting the ideals of former oppressors, though from a different vantage point. It entails rather a different design. It abandons, for instance, the view that brutality is the most manly and adaptability is the most womanly of all human traits.

Therefore emancipation does bring "disadvantages" to the man who sees himself robbed of his traditional privileges and who loses his unquestioned authority. But the goal of a mature and free society, built on partnership, includes provision for positive changes that are advantageous even for those in power. Isn't it conceivable that those who have been deprived of their toys and their slaves ought to be allowed to develop different needs than the well-known childish ones? What will otherwise become of the toy owners, slaveholders, and sex consumers when the objects of their dominance cease to be objects? The concept of emancipation implies progress not only for those who liberate themselves but equally for those who no longer have to live under the pressure of being rulers and consumers. But I am speaking of a dream, or rather a task that is waiting to be done—the dream of a more human society. This dream-task begins with two objectives which are the basis of every emancipation: self-criticism and criticism of society. Unfortunately I find that even today, after the emancipation has supposedly been accomplished, most women in our society still stand dumbfounded before these two objectives.

Instead of self-criticism we encounter either lamentation or self-glorification, a lot of loneliness on the one hand and a lot of "mother's day" on the other. In keeping with the stereotype, women in Germany ask two main questions which in some way are incorporated into every commercial and every ad: (1) How can I "get" one? (2) How can I "keep" him? The term "keep" is right on target, with its overtones of care for a dog or a piece of furniture. Many consider the spirit reflected in these questions to be perfectly normal; by all sorts of devices they try to keep it alive. Self-criticism could begin at this point.

And instead of criticism of society we find accommodation to the status quo. About forty years ago, Gertrud Bäumler, a German author, wrote that the full significance of the women's issue did not come to the fore until woman confronted a civilization in which she had no meaningful participation. The confrontation then was supposed to include criticism and revision, but what we ended up with were a few rights and complete accommodation. What was intended, dreamed, and sought was the big "Other," but the outcome was the big "Me Too." Thus, the emancipation of woman by way of social criticism can take place only if man will become liberated at the same time, only if he frees his consciousness from the modes of thinking which presently dominate it.

Theology has a part in shaping and determining these thought patterns, even for people who have a secular self-understanding. It is important to recognize under which god one has been socialized. The "male God" is a fundamental part of our culture. He is a being whose most important activity is rulership. Theologically, power becomes omnipotence, and rulership becomes world domination—total control and determination of all things, as at Auschwitz. The male God is the ruler of the universe, he has created the universe and has the power to intervene in it at any time. He is autonomous, totally independent of his creation. His rule is overall and he himself needs no one. This ruler derives neither stature nor happiness from having created any of us. He is, in theological terms, *aseity* (self-derived existence) raised to infinite power.

One must ask why people speak and think of God in terms of such *aseity* and omnipotence. In order to answer this question we may use the method developed by Ludwig Feuerbach. He holds that this God corresponds to a deep-seated fantasy of mankind. Men, too, wish to be self-sufficient, autonomous, dependent on no one. They too would like to be omnipotent rulers. Probably all of us, even women, have dreams of omnipotence, but these dreams find their verbal expression in the religion fabricated by men in the interest of men. The highest satisfaction men can imagine is to be autonomous and independent.

Actually, *Christian* faith can arise only if we dismiss this God once and for all. For if anything can be said with assurance about Christ—in contrast to this male God who is of course adored equally by many women—it is that Christ had no special prerogatives or privileges. Privileges are an integral part of the omnipotent male God; they are his essence. Christ, however, did not want any privileges; he abandoned them. In mythological language he left heaven, assumed servant's clothes, became vulnerable, hungry, thirsty, and mortal. The astronauts, when asked what God looked like, are reported—in a joke—to have answered, "She is black." When will we, all of us, begin to love and honor this God who is without power and rule? When will we rid ourselves of the male God and reach that point in faith where we can radically turn to Christ, without fear and without desire for special privilege? When will we be emancipated?

* * * * *

Translator's Epilogue

by Erdmut Mueller Brown

Dorothee Soelle is a young German political theologian who in the past decade has been continually among the creative avant-garde in new directions for theology. As her contributions to this volume show, she is not only acutely aware of but also personally involved in the issues which concern us in this book. Even though her major academic work and interest and most of her publications have been in the area of theology, her present faculty appointment at the University of Cologne is with the Institute of Germanic Philology rather than as a professor of theology. One might well speculate about the underlying sexism which has kept the male theologians in Germany from offering this obviously more-than-equal partner a chair in their circle.

Most notable perhaps about Ms. Soelle's theological concerns is the fact that she responds to her own theology with a kind of political activism which is uncommon in Germany. The most visible example of this "living theology" is probably the group known as Christians for Socialism (formerly Political Evening Prayers) which she organized and which provides the opportunity for making political and social concerns the center of worship.

The two poems included in this book were originally presented by the Political Evening Prayers in a service on "The Emancipation of Women" offered in Cologne on January 5 and 6, 1971. In a letter to one of the other contributors to this book, Dorothee Soelle explained that the poem "We Do Not Want" was the invitation to worship, and that the Mary poem was a meditation, which was spoken antiphonally after a lot of information and analysis had first been given about the exploitation of women from an economic and family point of view.

We took the liberty of separating the two poems because the first one seemed well-suited to introduce Part Two, and the Mary poem seemed an especially appropriate opening for Part Three. In regard to the Mary poem I might also mention that rather than translating the German Luther version of Luke, I have used the New English Bible version. I felt that the poem's intent of highlighting the contrast between the old and the new is best conveyed by this contemporary text.

As a sister in the struggle which comes to expression in this book, and as a translator, I feel particularly happy about Dorothee Soelle's contribution. Having grown up in Germany, with its outward freedom for university women and yet the unconscious mentality of the three Ks (*Kinder, Küche, Kirche*), I came to the States wondering what the new "American me" would be like, only to find that the most significant part of Americanization was fast becoming my involvement in the women's movement. This meant not only the pain and sometimes the joy of attempting the new in the here and now of my American family and social situation but also going back through much of the familiar mentality which informed my identity as a German woman. Thus change, for me, was due partly to a switch in cultures but more to a new vision which many of us share worldwide.

It was exciting for me to go back to Germany for Christmas in 1973, to see my own sisters, and to find that, though thousands of miles apart, we had gone through the same changes, and that they had brought us closer together than ever before. I am glad there are women like Dorothee Soelle who can give them support.

But beyond that, I believe that if our ultimate concern is for the liberation of all women, which I think it must be, then it is very important for us to be in touch with what women are doing all over the world. We need each other's support and we need to tell one another about different approaches in our respective cultures so that perhaps, some day, the most human possibility can become a reality.

14.

The Gifted Woman: New Style for Ministry

DOROTHY DONNELLY, CSJ

. . . he had no ax to grind and no uneasy male dignity to
defend; who took them as he found them and was completely
unselfconscious. There is no act, no sermon, no parable in the
whole Gospel that borrows its pungency from female perver-
sity; nobody could possibly guess from the words and deeds
of Jesus that there was anything "funny" about woman's
nature.

—Dorothy Sayers[1]

How you read Genesis depends on where
you're coming from. A friend of mine read it and said, "God
created man and he rested; then, he created woman and there's
never been any rest since!" Yes, it was a male friend who said
that. Another, though, also male, said that God created man,
took a good long look and knew he could do better: he created
woman.

Much of the repartee in male-female chauvinist discussions
today has a lighter tone than during the sixties, and that's a
blessing indeed. But this is for the very good reason I hope, that
women know much better now what they are about, what they
want, how easily they could be co-opted, and above all, how
easily they could be melted into the great technological, cultural blob of a decadent America.

Women involved in improving their status, self-image, working conditions, opportunities in education, politics, careers,
and the total culture, will for a time concentrate their energies

1. Dorothy Sayers, *Are Women Human?* (Downer's Grove, Ill.: Intervarsity
Press, 1971), p. 47.

88

on these fairly limited and definable targets. But eventually, I
trust, the goal of our effort will be full human liberation; involvement with our brothers in the battle for positive reform of
society, working for the family in mutuality and equality, pre-
ferring diversity to blind uniformity, complementarity to competition, and interdependence to separation. As Benjamin Barber puts it, women will be deeply and radically subversive of
Western society's institutionalized decadence, insisting that no
civilization can survive or remain free unless the human trinity
of woman, man, and child sanctifies its spirit.[2] Such an approach is much more arduous and, therefore, far less attractive.
Screaming at the enemy takes neither competence, wisdom,
nor insight. But challenging our culture—that is the real task. It
calls for our combined efforts against technocracy, simple-
mindedness, skepticism, greed, apathy, and despair. Barber
adds that women and men shall work together for such
freedom—through mutual struggle and sustained by mutual
love—or they shall never attain it at all.[3]

I believe him; moreover, I feel he is describing the major
cause of the so-called failure of Christianity. But G. K. Chester-
ton said Christianity has not failed—it has never been tried.
True, it has not been tried by 100 percent (*all* the men and
women) of the Christian church. Quite apart from our four-
hundred-year-old Protestant-Catholic argument so lately
ended, we have never, at any time, had the entire person-power
of all men and women in equality and collegiality prayerfully
discerning the gifts of the Spirit in themselves and others,
respecting them as his will, and humbly forming a community
of mutual love and service—never, except perhaps in Paul's
first communities which did include women like Phoebe in
positions of authority and influence.

A positive program for renewing American culture and the
Christian church will aim at justice, freedom, and love for *all*
men and women. It's goal will be *quality of life*. This is today
the aim of philosophy as well; it tries to enhance life in a world
where human experience is marked by alienation, incoher-

2. Benjamin Barber, "Man on Women," *Worldview*, May 1973, p. 54.
3. Ibid.

ence, and confusion. Both religion and philosophy have before them the task of renewal and reform in both church and society.

Church and society and their multimembered parts, if they want quality of life, have two choices before them: violence or imagination. I would opt for the latter. Enhancing the quality of life requires the use of intelligence seasoned by wisdom, the implementation of reason in prudent action. Above all, we will have to use the imagination God gave us for vision, for reflection, for seeing "what is not yet," for discerning conditions, within the cultural mutations forming the new value systems, for the possibility of human belief in Jesus as Lord. Here lies the root of the rejection of religion today: religion seems to have nothing to do with the quality of life.[4]

Through imagination, we Christians can show God to be constitutive of the human (man and woman); we can show how attention to God makes possible the full realization of the human. This approach will demand a new view of the human; one which assimilates and uses the masculine and the feminine principles consciously and with creative imagination. The real struggle for control of civilization is between w&men of imagination and w&men of violence (w&men = women and men). The former will know what the problem is and will act imaginatively to do something about it. They will not just shift positions and strategies in order to keep pace with changes in culture and views of reality, they will get out in front, ahead of such changes. This will call for a new kind of woman, a woman gifted with faithful imagination.

I find the prospect exciting for the future of women in ministry. Why? Because of some new approaches Christian teaching and practice have already made. I am thinking particularly of faith's new and imaginative major leap in its approach to the problem of life and to the conclusion of life, death. We have learned that by facing death in faith, we become free to give —and to serve! Indeed, it is in being loved and forgiven that faith becomes faith. The confrontation with death becomes an empowering:

4. Robert Johann, *The Pragmatic Meaning of God* (Milwaukee: Marquette University Press, 1966), p. 25.

> The Christian mind has mastered its own part of the problem
> of non-being by admitting a point of absolute non-being
> which can be called death . . . this complete impotence be-
> comes productive in man: e.g. the image of faith says that God
> seems attracted to the point of not-knowing in man, impo-
> tence of the mind. Faith uses this not-knowing. Hope has the
> same structure: impotence remains, as does weakness, but
> one hopes; . . . faith in the finite and in its last moment in death
> . . . doesn't keep us from guiding the city of man as well as that
> of God.[5]

God is attracted to powerlessness when imagination, used
fruitfully and faith-fully, changes powerlessness into capacity,
capacity for his power, his gifts. When faith lights up that
picture, new vision becomes possible. Women can begin to see
themselves as truly, in the best sense, "sons" of God who are
totally woman and totally human.

Seen in this light, the Incarnation can be related to the realization of the gifts of the Holy Spirit in Christian ministry in
church and society (even in the *ordained* priesthood or
ordained ministry). If ministry is related to mission as means to
end, and if the church fulfills its mission by ministering to
humankind as the sacrament of Christ in the world, then the
principle of pastoral ministry is, of course, the Incarnation. But,
if we understand the Son to have taken upon himself in that
Incarnation the totality of all humankind, men and women, and
so redeemed them, then my belief in the Incarnation also says
that I, a woman, have been taken up into Christ by his taking up
and redeeming of humankind, and that I too can die no more,
for through baptism and his gifts I have become part of his
Body, his church.

Then it follows, of course, that I am capable of receiving any
gift. I can fulfill any role or office in that church according to the
leading of the Spirit who gives me that call—and the community discerning that gift with me and in me, and confirming
it—if we so decide—in the sacrament of Holy Orders. Women,
then, as members of the Mystical Body of Christ, coheirs of the
kingdom, can be and are equally representative of Christ to the

5. William F. Lynch, *Continuum* 5, no. 3 (1967): 459.

world. The Equal Rights Amendment, of course, spells that
out in legislative and political language. However, the gospel
spelled it out long, long before that. Paul tried to implement it,
but no culture ever let it get through: "There is neither Jew nor
Greek, there is neither slave nor free, there is neither male nor
female; for you are all one in Christ Jesus" (Gal. 3:28). The
church, however, will confirm it in sacramental ordination for
those women with that call.

Imagine living in the first age and not only hearing those
words of Paul but being able to implement them! What a responsibility for women—through their intelligence, imagination, faith, justice, and love, to help build the new creation. And
what a long apprenticeship—two thousand years of preparation
in the West alone! Yet it has been a fruitful one in many ways,
for the subordination, inferior status, and powerlessness of
women have given us experiences of such worth that they
should never be forgotten in the years ahead, but never re-
called either in anger, revenge, or bitterness. (The men
around us also suffer from confusion, impotence, and despair
in the wake of cultural change.) I mean that powerlessness has
taught us to use imagination: how to think around, over, under, and often through a problem, obstacle, or situation, and to
conquer it—not by force or violence, but by intelligence, art or
artifice, and faith. Our long apprenticeship has been a painful
and sometimes crippling experience, but one with enormous
potential for the increase of understanding, forgiveness, and
reconciliation.

And the implementation is coming soon! The Work Group of
the University Ecumenical Institutes in Germany studied for
two years in ecumenical groups from the Reformed and
Catholic churches to provide a common ground for the theology of ministry of all Christians. Their report declares every
member of the faithful community a successor of the apostles
through the gift of service the Spirit has given w&men to
implement.[6] They agree that the authority of the early church
community was not necessarily given by the laying on of hands

6. "Reform und Anerkennung Kirchlicher Aemter," *Prospective*, Church
019/74 (Brussels, Belgium 1974).

(for bishops were not yet at the head of a group of local churches), but that it was continued by imposition of hands as a source of unity. They call ministry "service" in the tradition of the New Testament. Today that ministry will have to be very flexible, with old forms giving place to those the Spirit provides for meeting new needs in a new culture. Note that the report finds the point of control to reside in the community and in its service, each member using his or her own gifts humbly and prayerfully. This give and take implies personal conversion as the starting point of reform. This is what I meant when I referred to the spirit of understanding, forgiveness, and reconciliation which women with new powers can exercise, no matter what their new office or role.

The report also calls for the difficult task of faithful continuity to the message of Jesus—a continuous reorientation—radical continuity across cultural discontinuity. Actually, reform of ministry will call for four tasks: (1) diversification of ministry according to diversity of communities; (2) fundamental reappraisal of roles traditionally attributed to ministers, for example, freedom to choose a particular lifestyle: married or celibate, in a family or in a community; allowing married Catholic priests to continue their ministry; the possibility of priestly ministry being exercised conjointly with another profession for a limited period; (3) a reform of communication and decision-making processes in the church, which will still need government (but not a power structure marked by absolutism) so that all parts of the church can be heard from and listened to in policy making; (4) the German report's last-listed important reform: the exercise of ministry by women![7]

When we read that in the Catholic church the number of ordinations (men) fell 26 percent between 1965 and 1970 that last recommendation makes some sense. Women will be ordained, however, not only through their own earnest efforts, calls, requests, arguments, and studies, but also through the action of the Spirit—not only in calling women and giving them magnificent gifts, but also in seeming to call men in *other* directions no less fruitful for the church.

7. Ibid.

The picture of lady Marines landing on ecclesiastical beaches to shore up the failing ministry of the church is not a picture which attracts me. I agree with Krister Stendahl who insists that any thinking, any explanation which limits a maximum of equality in the church must be considered suspect, *even* that of including women in official ministry for the psychological or sociological benefits they would bring. Why? Because maximum equality is necessary for the full human existence of both women and men. "It is not good for the male to rule *by virtue* of his being male. His full humanity is at stake.[8] Nor, I add, for women to rush to the barricades by virtue of their being female, but only because they discern the call of the spirit of Jesus and have that call tested by the community and by their own experience, and confirmed by ordination.

When women are ordained I look forward to a new attitude on their part toward ministry. Ministry will be seen as being Christ in the world, Christ present and active in receiving, healing, sustaining, guiding, and reconciling. I see a new ministerial style, a new spirit of service, because of where women have been and where they want to go. The realization of the self-giving of the Father and the Son through the Spirit is integral to the very idea of ministry as service, but a service that shares life and love, and accepts life and love. How different from the all too common "cliff-stance" seen in clergymen as they "bend down" to the poor peons and disseminate light and information to the unenlightened, especially women.

Women in all times and places have had the same experience of physical femaleness, which usually involved powerlessness, no matter what the cultural environment. They learned well how to cope with powerlessness. Now they have to bring that experience into consciousness. Having experienced powerlessness for so long, women will also experience power. Many women fear the excesses of power, the corruption of authority. Some women, such as Sr. Ann Kelley, suggest that women shouldn't seek ordination because of the tradition of power and privilege associated with it in the past. I would agree with Don

8. Krister Stendahl, "Women in the Church" (Address delivered at Yale Divinity School, March 1970), printed in *Soundings*, 1970, p. 375.

Thorman's response to such a view: "Power is not evil always and should be accepted when it can be used for good; women should not be afraid of or shamed by the power of priesthood —they should seek to use and change it for the good of the church."[9]

By a new attitude, then, I don't mean refusing the power in policy and decision-making that will come with ordination to priesthood and ministry, but I do refer to the spirit and style of the ministry of women. Their only mortal sin will be to forget what it was like to be the underdog. Never should they fail to remember it in dealing with others, both men and women. Is the powerlessness of our past to be remembered simply because of the psychological or sociological benefits of such a stance? No, but because the richest fruits of our new style and service will spring from its deep theological roots: imitation of the death-accepting, death-defying ministry of the powerless Jesus.

To be the underdog means to be identified with the underdog of every society in history—the poor. The experience of limitedness, powerlessness, needingfulness belongs especially to the poor, but it is also the existential condition of all men and women before God. Paul has marvelously reflected upon the dynamic of weakness and power in Christianity, but like his assertion of male-female equality, the "acceptable time" seems never to have arrived for the interiorization and implementation of that concept. In our American tradition of independence, self-support, and rugged individualism, the idea of being a receiver—a gifted one, the beneficiary of spontaneous, unmotivated, value-creating love—seems foreign indeed. Is it possible that women in a position to proclaim the gospel can do something more meaningful with that concept, *agape*, the gift of the Father and the Son—their Spirit? For, receiving *agape*, God's unconditioned love, is the *condition* of ministry. He hath first loved us, empowered us with his Spirit so that we can love one another. In fact, the ability to accept myself as loved, to share *and* receive gifts in serving the com-

9. Donald Thorman, "Women Priests," *National Catholic Reporter* 17 (August 1973): p. 10.

munity, is proof of being empowered, of being loved by such a love as Theirs.

The "careful critical contemplation of the condition of men"[10] is an important aspect of ministry. It involves awareness of need, vision, reflection, and interpretation. But I feel that women may well add the dimension of depth to the realization of whence comes this power of ministry, whence comes the ability to cause change in self and in others—from the spirit of Jesus. (Not that men have not known this; they have not had equal opportunity to experience it from a position of powerlessness—where it really means something different.) It is this style I hope for in women, this being willing to accept myself as gift of the Trinity, to accept myself as I am: limited, sinful, imperfect. "I'm *not* OK, and *that's* OK"—because of the spirit of Jesus. Then there are no "cliff-stances," but a receiving and a sharing; then I can accept and love others as they are, not as I would require them to become, for I must love them as Jesus loves me.

The source of ministry, then, is found in the Lord. Ministering becomes the exercise of influence in a given situation through receiving love, visioning, listening, and challenging through the power of the Holy Spirit, all based upon accepting the other as other, and a dying to the desire for power over others that is alien to that Spirit. The answer to whose influence, whose power it should be is, of course, *Theirs*.

This attitude, style, and approach can radically change the manner of ministering. It can lead quickly to team ministry with its discerning of and respect for the gifts of all w&men in the community, and ultimately to a great expansion of ministry to include many forms of ordination, not only to priesthood, but to ministeries for married w&men, celibate brothers and sisters, and single people. This means really taking the Holy Spirit seriously. It also means being serious about prayer, not as daily mumbling, but as daily listening, listening to each person —especially those to whom I minister—as a messenger of the

10. Henri Nouwen, *Creative Ministry* (New York: Doubleday & Co., 1971), p. 63.

Spirit, a bearer of his word to me. In the Spirit's exquisite economy, these persons will surely be the ones who minister to me. Ministry for women may be a model of mutual gift giving and receiving which could revolutionize the total ministry of the people of God. In the words of a distinguished colleague of mine: "If ministry is not exercising influence through, with, and in the Spirit, it is not ministry."[11]

Finally, women will be called to exercise ministry in a spirit of faith-full imagination which will refuse to see violent means as the primary answer to any problem. I would hope we are now ready to use our rich experience of thinking indirectly, intuitively, and imaginatively so that all of us, w&men, can solve society's problems in a more intelligent, creative, and faith-full fashion. Maybe we will even let the loving light and creative might of the Spirit in on the act—which, after all, is his act, his creation. That approach would call for the demise of the love of power and the birth of the power of love—himself. Teilhard de Chardin felt that we had conquered for God the winds and the waves and the tides (and now, outer space!). Could we now not conquer for God the most dynamic power on the face of the earth, the power of love—and then, for the second time in the history of the world w&men shall have discovered—FIRE!

11. George B. York, "Ministering: Journey into Meaning" (M. Th. diss., Jesuit School of Theology at Berkeley, 1973), p. 91.

15.

Let Her Works
Praise Her

CLARE BENEDICKS FISCHER

The title of this chapter, taken from the song in praise of the hardworking woman of Proverbs 31, echoes the scriptural call to honor woman's work. In antiquity, the community affirmed "in the gates" the labors of the persevering Hebrew wife, thus symbolically reconciling the private and public spheres of work. It is this vision of unity, with its recognition of the dignity and value of womanpower, which I wish to underscore in my assessment of the contemporary work ethic.

Until comparatively modern times, home and work place were not separated, and the imagery we have today of gender and place was unknown. There is no doubt that the sexual division of labor spans centuries, but the merger of masculine identity with the idea of going from the hearth, and of feminine identity with staying at home is less than three hundred years old. Yet, this association has proven to be tenacious and, perhaps, the greatest obstacle to an authentically egalitarian society. Despite the fact that the utilization of women in the labor force has increased rapidly in the last three decades, the prescriptive authority of "a woman's place" has not dramatically changed. In a recent economic analysis of job satisfaction[1] one author notes that with the erosion of the traditional sexual division of labor by shifts in the work population, he fears that male work motivation may be in jeopardy. Masculinity and successful providing reinforce one another, both requiring that

1. Daniel Yankelovich, "The Meaning of Work," *The Worker and the Job*, ed. Jerome Rosow (New Jersey: Prentice-Hall, 1974).

98

the woman assume material dependence upon her spouse. This relationship of male responsibility and female dependence implies that the wife remain at home and be looked after. While research in the ethics of work reveals the persistence of the traditional dichotomy between home and work, it identifies the growing reality of the "working woman." Economists cannot disregard the rapid rise of the female labor force since the end of the Second World War. However, they fret about the postindustrial society in which resources are no longer inexhaustible and progress is not infinite. Is it not absurd that the potential of woman's energy continues to go unrecognized?

Although the social scientist leaves us with some unsettling conclusions about contemporary trends, we would hope that the theologian would readily identify the positive aspects of woman's changing role. In the past twenty years a new theology, known under the rubric of "theology of work" has emerged.[2] Contributors to this theological discussion talk about the humanization of life and about the realization of self through work. But they write as if woman's activity in economic and cultural terms is either nonexistent or limited to the reproductive and nurturing functions. They ignore the role of women in building the earth, implying that the implementation of equality in the work force might effectively disrupt family life and jeopardize human purpose.

A theology of work must include an account of woman's contribution and potential. It must discover and lay to rest those powerful myths which perpetuate the idea of woman's secondary role. It must inform and educate everyone about woman's share in the creation of a progressively better life. Traditional approaches cannot illuminate our present circumstances. We are too far removed from the expectations and life-styles of antiquity to subscribe to a purely scriptural view of human activity. Three analytical approaches are here sug-

2. Among the titles are: M.D. Chenu, *The Theology of Work* (Chicago: H. Regnery and Co., 1963); Louis Savary, *Man, His World and His Work* (New York: Paulist Press, 1967); J.H. Oldham, *Work in Modern Society* (Richmond: John Knox Press, 1961).

gested which can provide orientation and guide us toward a
more humane condition: the penitential, the creationist, and
the eschatological.

THE GARDEN: WORK AS PENANCE

The memory of the lost garden, that paradise where all goods
were harvested effortlessly, infuses what we are calling the
"penitential" theology of work with a mood of remorse. Based
upon the Genesis myth, work—on this view—is understood as
a curse, a consequence of the primal act of disobedience. To
redeem the conditions of the garden, thistles and thorns must
be uprooted with great pain and frustration in order to make
way for the consumable. The necessities for human survival are
to be gleaned only through incessant toil. Human history after
the Fall is a restless record of an irksome coping with the
resistant; a confrontation with the unruly weeds which glut the
garden and detract from order. Until elusive nature succumbs
to human governance work will not end.

The justification for a separation of human work roles on the
basis of divine ordinance, however, cannot be derived from
either of the creation narratives of Genesis; both point to the
unitary nature of the obligation to tend the garden. In Genesis
1:28-31 male and female are enjoined to "be fruitful," to "sub-
due" and "have dominion" over the earth together, and the
woman of Genesis 2:15-23 is man's partner in Eden. Only with
the breach of authority, with the symbolic ingestion of the
forbidden fruit, does a division of labor emerge. But even in the
discharge of the curse (Gen. 3:16-18) no authority is given for a
separation of capacities according to sexual identity. A rigid
formulation of distinctive spheres of activity emerges, rather,
with a penitential theology of work. With its compulsion to
order, to secure mastery over an elusive nature, it sets about
dispelling ambiguities and disharmonies. It understands a dis-
tinction in function—productive and reproductive—to be an
application of a natural law grounded on biological difference.
Accordingly, any deviance from this bipolar organization of
work represents a reenactment of the original sin. So men *must*
go forth from the hearth, and women *must* remain at home with

the children. Despite this theological attempt to regulate the
domains of human effort in order to prevent cosmic disharmonies, human history has not kept the work roles of men and
women that neatly separated; innumerable women have also
worked for their bread by the sweat of their brows.

Two myths, which represent obstacles to woman's right to
gainful employment today, reflect this penitential theology of
work. Both lose credence in face of the social facts.

The first myth asserts, ostensibly on a biological basis, that
women have a singular purpose—the care and maintenance of
their families. But one need only refer to the Old Testament to
disprove this myth. The woman of Proverbs 31, whose "works
praise her," engages in a number of tasks that take her away
from the home, including marketing and real estate; she performs these tasks clothed in "strength and dignity."

In a comprehensive study of women and work[3] we find
ample evidence that women were involved in productive work
throughout history, until the time of the Industrial Revolution.
Many of the tasks which had been women's responsibilities in
an earlier age, tasks such as spinning and soap-making, were
then assumed by men in a factory setting. Only gradually have
women, in their struggle for employment opportunities, begun
to secure these work tasks again.

The current effort of women is to demonstrate the viability of
combining work and home commitments. A glance at the statistical record indicates that the female labor force has doubled
since 1940, with more than 33 million women in the work force
as of 1972. This number represents 42 percent of the adult
female population of the United States, and 38 percent of the
total labor force. The most dramatic change has come with the
eightfold increase of working mothers in less than thirty years.
Over 50 percent of the female labor force have responsibility
for children between the ages of six and seventeen. Twenty-
nine percent of all white women workers, and 47 percent of all
minority women workers, have children under six.

3. Alva Myrdal and Viola Klein, *Women's Two Roles, Home and Work* (London:
Routledge and Kegan Paul, 1956).

A more recent myth is that of homemaking as a "career." In
our culture the activity of running a home is clothed in an
illusive professionalism. It requires, according to Myrdal and
Klein, that the housewife integrate in her person an "unholy
alliance" between Eden's work ethic of productivity and its
imagery of leisure. She must be continuously busy, expending
up to as much as sixty hours a week on household duties but,
buttressed by the media's vision of the lady of leisure, she must
work just as hard to be sleek, beautiful, and glamorous. In short,
the career homemaker is superwoman—she overcomes all the
contradictions between drudgery and efficiency, routine and
adventure. Her education comes from popular culture
—magazines, television advertisements, and soap opera role-
models provide innumerable examples of successful women
and their "tips." In this breathless world of the professional
housewife we glimpse the penitential imagery of work as
"keeping order"—her career triumphs are the dissolution of all
dirt and the overcoming of physical and familial disarray.

Theologians writing about work usually distinguish the
Hebrew from the Greek view, emphasizing the elitism and
competitiveness of the latter. To be sure, the ancient Greeks
looked upon manual labor with disdain and gladly delegated
onerous responsibilities in order to free themselves to be citizens of the polis. The modern housewife similarly frees her
family to function outside the home without trivial distractions.
However, the Greeks did not originate competitive activity.
Hebrew sources, according to one biblical scholar,[4] indicate
that competition is a consequence of fratricide. The narrative of
Cain and Abel (Gen. 4:2-9) offers a symbolic account of the
jealousy and rivalry which lead to sibling murder. The implications of this act, paralleling the Fall of man, are an accursed
condition and a history of strife between brothers and sisters.
For women in a patriarchal culture, the results of original sin
and of Cain's homicide have been domination and division.

The penitential theology of work instructs us that redemp-
tion is dependent upon remedial activity. Our work is to repair

4. Alan Richardson, *The Biblical Doctrine of Work* (London: SCM Press,
1952).

our relationships with others and with the earth. One imperative for constructive change is to right the imbalances which have reigned throughout history. Male sovereignty in the productive spheres of human life must be countered with enhanced female participation—not dominance but equality according to Charlotte Perkins Gilman: "There is before us no overturning, no attempt at a new domination of women over men.... It is not a contest between them, but a recognition of a common hope, a common power, a common duty."[5]

THE COMMUNITY: CREATION AND WORK

The optimism of a "creationist" approach to the theology of work contrasts dramatically with the disciplined assertiveness of the penitential view. Whereas the penitential view stressed the brokenness and lostness that characterizes the disobedient nature of humans, the creationist or "incarnational" perspective, deriving also from the Genesis myth, focuses instead upon the wholeness of creation and the proclivity to share and tend. Humankind is made in God's image (Gen. 1:27) and its authentic expression is symbolized in the divine magnanimity and cooperative spirit of the garden (Gen. 1:28). To participate in the creative order, humans work, and this work is an expression of solidarity and service. We find this idea reiterated in the Gospel parables (especially Matt. 25) and Pauline epistles (Gal. 6:2) of the New Testament.

On this creationist view, work is "right and proper." Human identity is inseparable from it and correlates with the effort expended, in community, in the ongoing, progressive, collaborative construction of the earthly city. The example of the female ant (Prov. 6:6-8) provides a model of productivity; she requires no external authority or motivation: "consider her ways and be wise." Failure, then, is idleness, or such work as derives from negative motivation rather than positive desire. Paul warns the Thessalonians that the new covenant does not imply abandonment of earthly endeavors—to shirk self-

5. Charlotte Perkins Gilman, *His Religion and Hers* (New York: Century Co., 1923), pp. 279-80.

responsibility for the tasks of this world is to lose sight of human purpose (2 Thess. 3:7-12).

The creationist approach again suggests two highly debilitating myths about women's work. Both myths deny the seriousness of purpose or the significance of meaning which might otherwise be embraced in the divine scheme. Female labor is regarded as derivative and trivial. At the core of the argument is disbelief in woman's capacity to be motivated, or to make commitments on her own. Women are assumed to be lacking a zest for building the earth, except when authority directs or supports their endeavors.

The first of these two myths offers the stereotype of the woman worker who labors in the job market only to *supplement* her family's income. Supposedly, her motivation is entirely dependent upon others' needs, and her own commitment is partial, insignificant, and unreliable. But the motivation of the working woman needs to be assessed in the light of the facts.

It has been estimated that nearly nine out of ten American women will seek work for a wage at some point in their lives. On the average they will work for twenty-five years and their reasons for doing so are not for "pin money" or incidental motives. "The majority of women do not have the option of working solely for personal fulfillment."[6] This includes, as of 1972: 7.5 million single women; 6.2 million widowed, divorced, and separated women who are raising children; and more than 7 million women whose husbands did not earn adequate incomes to provide for their families.

Approximately one-third of the women workers in the United States work because they *must*—they are *not* derivative, they do *not* supplement, they *provide*. A recent survey of European women workers, reported in the American press, indicated that one-half of those interviewed identified economic necessity as the reason for employment.[7]

The other myth, a corollary one, is that housewifery is preferred by modern women because it makes so few demands

6. Data from "Why Women Work," Women's Bureau, Employment Standards Administration, U.S. Dept. of Labor, Washington, D.C., 1973.
7. *Women Today* 4 (15 April 1973): 51.

upon their time. It posits the idle wife and mother who, thanks to technology, has little to do, but visit with her friends, watch television, and indulge her natural predisposition to be passive and lazy.

John Galbraith's thesis, however, that the modern housewife is a "crypto-servant," an unpaid domestic who manages the home and generates a progressively expanding rate of consumption, dispels the idea of indolence. Arguing from an expertise in economics, he describes how the housewife performs her menial labors without wages because she has been deluded by the notion of "convenient social virtue." Her tireless, though uncompensated housework is valued at more than $13,000 a year. Her most important function, however, is that of wisely buying in the marketplace, managing the goods of capitalist production, no small task for the indolent.

> "... in their crypto-servant role of administrators [they] make an indefinitely increasing consumption possible. As matters now stand (and for as long as they so stand), it is their supreme contribution to the modern economy."[8]

The creationist understanding of work is, after all, companionship in service. Neither the myth of deficient motivation nor the myth of prevailing indolence communicate the isolation and alienation of the woman worker. If she is responsible for the support of her family as well as its management (housework), she has little time or energy for sociability. On the other hand, her sense of performing *only* household labor often keeps her in a frenzied state. Ms. Myrdal and Ms. Klein note:

> ... there is sufficient evidence to justify the suspicion that housewives often unconsciously expand it [housework] in order to allay their feelings of frustration by providing evidence that they are fully occupied and indispensable.[9]

Woman's feeling of being an accessory rather than a principal in the creation of human history can be dispelled only at that juncture in time and place where recognition is open, and

8. John Kenneth Galbraith, *Economics and the Public Purpose* (Boston: Houghton Mifflin Co., 1973), p. 37.
9. Myrdal and Klein, *Women's Two Roles*, p. 37.

the myopia of cultural vision is corrected by "work-human-ship." "The closeness of that sort of community grows to the extent that labor not only demands mutual respect and care, but also the combination of each one's contribution to the same teamwork."[10]

PROMISE: WORK AS FULFILLMENT

Besides the penitential approach and the creationist view, a third—an eschatological—perspective is offered. Theologians who speak of the subject of work from this perspective give it a christocentric emphasis. The reference is not to the experience of the man Jesus, but to the mystery of Christ's mission on earth—that ambiguity of presence and otherness. The disjunction of human experience and transcendent purpose is overcome by an act of faith. Ultimate significance and authentic completion must await the Second Coming, but humans cannot defer their personal quest for meaning to an indefinite tomorrow. So, in sharing in that mystery of the "end," and fathoming its permeation into all things and events present, persons are able to take comfort in, and secure assurance from, their earthly endeavors. Both the message of John 4:34, where Jesus' nourishment is obtained in fulfillment of the divine work, and of Paul ("in him all things hold together," [Col. 1:17]), inform this approach.

From the point of view of women's experience, the eschatological perspective is the most promising, assuring an integration of persons such as heretofore has never been realized in human history. The low self-esteem of working women is well known. Their ability to escape the fetters of role assignment is only beginning to be put to the test.

> Work is more than a bread-and-butter issue. Our self-esteem and dignity are functions of the work we perform. Sexual or role stereotyping has not only inhibited the development of women's economic power, but has robbed women of the self-esteem, dignity, confidence in their innate abilities.[11]

10. Peter Schoonenberg, *God's World in the Making* (Pittsburgh: Duquesne University Press, 1964), p. 156.
11. Lucille Rose, in *Report of Proceedings*, "Women's Work" conference, The New School, New York, September 1973.

The motif of fulfillment on this eschatological view stands in opposition to two more myths about female labor. Both represent ways of seeing woman as non–self-determining. And again their credibility is shaken by the facts. The first myth focuses on female aptitudes and the distortion in occupational aspiration and actual work assignment. The woman worker is said to be intellectually inept for, or physically incapable of, certain jobs. Her talents and capacities are defined by traditional stereotypes about the work place.

Statistical analysis of occupational categories, of course, demonstrates the obvious—that most women who work for a wage are employed in repetitious, low-skilled positions requiring only minimal education or training. In brief, the female "employment ghetto" is composed of women whose individuality is at a low premium; they can be easily replaced and they function in service positions. One and a half million women work as domestics, earning less than $2,000 a year; 34 percent of the employed female labor force expends its energy on tedious clerical jobs, another 17 percent on factory assembly lines, and at least 8 percent on their feet as sales personnel.

What these facts patently indicate is simply the tremendous waste of women's abilities as persons. There is something askew when 20 percent of the women who have completed four years of college are employed in clerical positions and only 16 percent of the female labor force is classified as being professional (a category which includes traditional service jobs such as nursing, teaching, and librarianship).

The second myth assumes an inherent unreliability among women workers. It focuses on their presumably high rate of job turnover and absenteeism, and regards them as poor risks in the employment market. Women are said to be indifferent and to lack commitment to their work. This myth of unreliability argues that women's biological "vulnerabilities" and familial responsibilities augment these disabilities. Although the facts of women's home distractions cannot be denied, there is considerable evidence that women work with as much consistency as men when job inducements are equal.

Perhaps the most jarring aspect of this myth is its implicit

support of the statistical reality of unequal pay scales. Despite
the move for "equal pay for equal work," the gap widens. Eli
Ginzberg reports that women earn approximately less than
three-fifths as much as men.[12]

Obviously, inequitable remuneration and minimal inducements contribute substantially to job abandonment and absenteeism. At the same time, these factors reinforce the woman
worker's depressed view of her own economic value.

The theological implications of this waste are apparent when
we turn again to the eschatological notion of completion,
fulfillment. Feelings of futility in employment, and in unem-
ployment, negate one's sense of sharing in the "becoming" of
the earth. To the extent that women are locked out of responsible positions, and undervalued in the ones which they have,
their sense of participation in the ultimate task creation
—remains one-sided. This seems especially true when the
figures of black unemployed women and the poverty levels of
minority families are considered. Ginzberg notes, "Of the
families with female heads who worked year-round, full-time,
Negroes were four times more likely than whites to be caught
in poverty!"[13]

Society is deprived of an immeasurable potential when it
closes the doors to female participation in all facets of its work.
Every woman is deprived when from her earliest years she is
prevented from aspiring to and striving for what she could
become, prevented by prescribed stereotypes, restraints of behavior, and limitations of education and occupation. When
woman's work one day unfolds into the creative expression it
must become if it is to contribute authentically to the
fulfillment and wholeness of the human endeavor, then sus-
picions about intellect and reliability will be dispelled in the
knowledge that all humankind thrives "for the sake of doing
well a thing that is well worth doing."[14]

Among the countless approaches to the question of work,

12. Eli Ginzberg, "Introduction," in Robert Smuts, *Women and Work in
America* (New York: Schocken, 1971), p. ix.
13. Ibid., p. x.
14. Dorothy Sayers, quoted in Oldham, *Work in Modern Society*, p. 52.

and the examination of woman's role in the modern economy,
there is a valuable perspective emerging from the theological
view of women's work. Theologically, we may perceive three
relationships derived from the three approaches (penitential,
creationist, and eschatological) taken here. These relationships
define our presence and purpose in the world in terms of the
"garden," the "community," and the "future." The first refers
to natural resources; the second, to human resources; and the
last, to our mutual responsibility for human history. They offer
a simple guide to a more holistic existence:

1. we are persons who in reverence must tend and care for all
   nature;
2. we are persons in a relationship with one another which
   demands loving community;
3. we are persons in a relationship with one another which
   calls for attentiveness.

These three relationships necessarily lead to concrete programs of action—to vocational and continuing education,
child-care services, modifications in maternity and pregnancy
policies; and encouragement to participate and take leadership
in unions—programs which will effect the changes needed to
bring about an attentive, caring humanity. Both the material
and psychological circumstances of women's work must be
transformed to assure humankind that human history is really
worth it.

> Something must be wrong in a social organization in which
> men may die a premature death from coronary thrombosis, as
> a result of overwork and worry, while their wives and widows
> organize themselves to protest their lack of opportunities to
> work.[15]

15. Myrdal and Klein, *Women's Two Roles*, p. 186.

16.

Human Liberation Waits

ANNE McGREW BENNETT

If there is any one word which could be used to describe the hopes of almost every person today it is the word "liberation." Liberation from whatever limits self-fulfillment. Liberation from the barriers that prevent the exercise of freedom. Liberation, that is, from economic, social, political, racial, and sexist exploitation and oppression. Liberation movements deal with, and challenge, the very foundations of present-day personal and social life. However, "liberation" has become a slogan and the details of the vision are often vague and blurred.

We approach this subject, human liberation, as women claiming full personhood for all women. This is difficult, for we are not representative of all women. Women are young, old, rich, poor, black, white, well, ill—women are of every nation, every ethnic group, every religious and social group. No woman's experience encompasses the experiences of all women. And yet, as we reflect on the vision of human liberation and on the barriers that bind and limit woman, each of us must try to "feel" what it means to be woman seeking to be person today, not just in our own personal life, but as every-woman.

It is commonplace to say that we live in a society that is both racist and sexist. But to speak in condemnation of such a society personally and in official church statements is not enough. The movement for human liberation must deal with the causes of racism and sexism: thought patterns, beliefs, and commitments which are dominant in society and which, therefore, mold and shape not only the individual life of each person but our entire culture.

110

As we think about the Western world and try to understand why women here have been denied full personhood, we are faced with the fact that for thousands of years woman's life has been molded by the Judeo-Christian tradition. And, because of the power and dominance of the European and North American nations, people in all parts of the world are deeply influenced by the Judeo-Christian tranditions even if they are not Jews or Christians. The Scriptures are of central importance because they have been, and are, regarded as revealing the very nature and purposes of God and, therefore, of humankind. In searching for the roots of discrimination against women we find that women who appear in the vast sweep of biblical stories and in their interpretations have an inferior status in the relational structure of men and women. The Old Testament story is about men, fathers and sons: Adam, Cain, Abel, Noah, Abraham, Isaac, Jacob, Joseph, Moses, the kings, the prophets. Sometimes a wife or daughter or sister is mentioned but usually in terms of a derivative relationship with a man. In the New Testament the emphasis is also on men who are related in some way to God's revelation in Jesus of Nazareth: the shepherds, the wise men from the East, the twelve apostles, Paul and the leaders of the early church. Almost all of the women who are mentioned are identified by their relationship to men: the Virgin Mother, mothers, sisters, wives, widows, prostitutes, daughters.

The real issue facing women who are struggling to be "free to be human" is the dominance of men over women. This leads inevitably to women's "inferiority" and men's "superiority." The dominance of men over women has had a long, long history. In our own culture the pervasiveness of this dominance is so total that like the air about us we have difficulty "seeing" it. Our language refers to humankind as "he, him, his" and omits woman who is half of humankind. Our customs in marriage and family rites keep men and women unequal; men are honored as the "head," woman's identity is subservient. Our laws, political institutions, and economic systems discriminate in favor of men. Our written histories, secular and religious, are almost entirely about the great men of history and their activities, especially their wars and theological controversies. Woman's history is hidden history.

It is important as we reflect on human liberation to keep in mind that the "inferiority" of women in our culture is an inferiority of rights and of power which is embodied in customs, laws, and theories. Women, in our country, have been trying since before the founding of our Republic to be recognized as full citizens "with all the rights and duties thereto." The Constitution and bylaws of the United States did not so recognize women. The amendments after the Civil War which gave the black male suffrage rights and equal protection under the law did not include black or white women. Even though women finally got the vote in 1920, women are still struggling to get the Equal Rights Amendment passed. The E.R.A. is subject, of course, to approval by the men who control all of the legislative, judicial, and executive bodies of government and the communications media.

Our churches and religious institutions are also male-led and male-dominated even though the majority of the members are women. Women in the Christian church have long been trying to be recognized as full human beings, "made in the image of God," and to be given an opportunity to minister in whatever capacity they feel called. What is there about our Judeo-Christian heritage which supports the dominance of men over women?

The most important element in understanding a culture is its idea of divinity. The Bible came out of a patriarchal society. God is "He." *Yahweh* is the God of Abraham, Isaac, and Jacob who knew him as *El-Shaddai*, a male God (Exod. 6:2-3). Israel also drew from her own experience a number of names for God to express her faith: Father, Brother, Kinsman, King, Judge, Shepherd—all male names. The legal codes of Israel treat woman primarily as chattel. In the New Testament Paul is quoted as considering women subordinate to their husbands (1 Cor. 14:34-35; 1 Tim. 2:11-15). Scholars question the authenticity of these passages but they are widely used to deny woman's equality. 1 Timothy 2:13-14 makes woman responsible for sin in the world.

The extreme male-centeredness of biblical writers, especially editors, is shown in the hundreds of incidents throughout the Hebrew Bible in which feminine words have been changed to masculine in order to express reverence for the holy. All Hebrew words are either masculine or feminine gender. Feminine words referring to sacred objects or having to do with worship have been changed to masculine; for example, the golden dishes on the altar, the bread, curtains, rings, doorposts, and candlesticks. Even the milk cows that brought back the Ark are referred to as masculine six times! One research scholar comments, "We may formulate the following principle: whenever someone or something attained an unusual or elevated status, whether temporary or permanent, the Scribes used masculine pronominal suffixes with reference to feminine words."[1]

If the above statements are all, or the essence, of what biblical religion means, then women are in a very bad situation. We have little hope of claiming whole personhood as long as the male-dominated Judeo-Christian traditions mold our understanding of God/Creation/Man/Woman.

Fortunately, there is another approach to the Bible. The Bible and biblical tradition can be reread, keeping in mind the patriarchal bias of the writers and redactors and interpreters, in an effort to understand our biblical faith without sexist blinders.

We can reflect, for example, on the meaning of personhood for men and women in the ancient story of the creation of humankind: "So God created man in his own image; in the image of God he created him; male and female he created them . . ." (Gen. 1:27). This verse has been interpreted quite differently for men than for women. There is no question in the minds of men who follow the Judeo-Christian faith but that men are created in God's image with all the dignity and power and "superiority" that that means. As for women, it has been widely taught and believed that because they are not male they are an inferior creation.

1. Mayer G. Slonim, "The Substitution of the Masculine for the Feminine Pronominal Suffixes to Express Reverence," *Jewish Quarterly Review* 29 (1938-39): 397-403.

But reread the story. Begin with the previous verse: "Then
God said, 'Let us make man in our image, after our like-
ness....'" Notice that in this passage the writer does not have
God say "Let us make man in *my* image," but "in *our* image."
The Hebrew word for God in these passages is not *Yahweh* or
El which are masculine singular nouns used to refer to God.
The Hebrew word is *Elohim.* It is a plural word which is used
in the Bible to refer to the God of Israel and to other gods, both
male and female.[2] Scholars, most of them male of course, have
a great deal of trouble with the word *Elohim.* Some of them try
to ignore the plural and dismiss it as the plural of majesty.
However, Dean Cuthbert A. Simpson, who is the exegete in
The Interpreter's Bible for the elucidation of these particular
passages in the creation story in which *Elohim* is used, writes:
"The creation of man is invested with a special solemnity....
What seems to be significant is the idea that for the creation of
man it was fitting, if not necessary, that there should be something like co-operation on the part of the whole company of
heaven."[3]

Another problem for us in this passage, as we think about
women, is the use of the word "man": "God created man."
The Hebrew word translated "man" in this passage is a generic
term, not a male term. It should be translated "persons,"
"humankind," or some other generic term, not "man" which
may mean "male" and always carries a male image.

We all know how language limits and determines thought.
How much difference there would be in our understanding of
personhood if in the creation story the word *Elohim* were used
throughout for the word "God" and the referent masculine
pronouns, and if the generic term "persons" were used instead
of "man"! "Elohim said, 'Let us create persons in our image,
after our likeness' ... So Elohim created persons in Elohim's
own image ... male and female Elohim created them."

The ancient creation story, in profound symbolism, de-

2. Alan Richardson, ed., *A Theological Word Book of the Bible* (New York:
Macmillan Co., 1951), pp. 94-99; *The Interpreter's Dictionary of the Bible*
(New York and Nashville: Abingdon Press, 1962), 2:407-17.
3. *The Interpreter's Bible* (New York and Nashville: Abingdon Press, 1952),
1:482-83.

scribes God as inclusive being, and all persons as made in God's image. The story is universal in scope. There are no inferior persons. Woman is portrayed the same as man, "made in the image of God." Both are persons, sex is secondary. Familiar translations blur the meaning.

The second chapter of Genesis contains another creation myth which is formative in our understanding of "woman's place." According to the usual interpretation of this story woman was made after man to be a helper for him. It is best not to be too literal in interpreting myths. However, the word translated as "helpmeet" or "helper" is the Hebrew word used of divine, or superior, help. The word never refers to inferior help in the Bible.

Probably the story (myth) most often quoted over the thousands of years to justify keeping woman inferior to man is the story of the Fall. Eve (whose name, by the way, means "Life" or "Mother of all living") and Adam are still in the Garden of Eden. They have eaten of the forbidden fruit and God says to Eve, according to modern translators of this story: "I will greatly multiply your pain in childbearing; in pain you shall bring forth children, yet your desire shall be for your husband, and he shall rule over you" (Gen. 3:16). Modern scholars' comments on this passage are most interesting—and very different from the common interpretation! Dean Simpson writes:

> Most significant is the fact that [the writer] far in advance of his time sees that this domination of woman by man is an evil thing. The implication is that the relationship between husband and wife was intended by God to be a mutual and complementary relationship of love and respect, not a relationship in which one dominated the other.[4]

Dr. Phyllis Trible, an Old Testament scholar, writes: "This statement is not license for male supremacy, but rather it is condemnation of that very pattern."[5]

4. Ibid., p. 510.
5. "Depatriarchalizing in Biblical Interpretation," *Journal of the American Academy of Religion*, March 1973, p. 41.

A literal translation of the ancient Greek version of this passage found in the Septuagint reads quite differently from our translations: "Unto the woman [God] said, a snare hath increased thy sorrow and thy sighing; Thou art turning away [from God] to thy husband, and he will rule over thee."[6] In this translation it is very clear that woman is being warned against depending on her husband rather than on God.

Surely biblical scholars know that the translation in our Bible implies a false interpretation. This is obvious from their commentaries, but few people have access to these corrective interpretations. Many an article and sermon have extolled "woman's place" as "helper" to her husband, not to mention statements blaming woman for bringing sin into the world and justifying treatment of women as inferior persons and second-class citizens. Half the human race—men—grow up with an exalted ego because God and humankind are always referred to by their identification, by the use of masculine nouns and pronouns, while woman is referred to as man's "helpmeet." What violence these interpretations have done, and continue to do, to both women and men! How do we go about overcoming this destructive pattern of life?

First, women must insist on rereading and reinterpreting the old myths in the Bible. Our faith is passed on from generation to generation through myths and symbols. When a particular culture has distorted the meaning of the myths and symbols which mold our lives, then those myths and symbols must be reinterpreted so that they no longer perpetuate discrimination and oppression.

Women must also insist that women be accorded their rightful place in history. It is the past on which a person depends to build a self-identity. Historians recognize the fateful importance of the way the past is interpreted. The British historian J. H. Plumb emphasizes the fact that history is not the past. He points out that the past is a created ideology in order to control and motivate societies, individuals, and classes.

6. Katherine C. Bushnell, *God's Word to Women* (Oakland, Calif.: The Author, 1923), sec. 114-45.

If an easily identifiable group is portrayed as never having made any general contributions to society—that is, if their contributions are always thought of as within one very limited sphere (with women this would be giving birth and nurturing the family)—then that group of persons are thought of as "other" and the dominant group in the culture continues to hold them in an inferior, usually servant role. Oppressed groups often come to accept the second-class, subservient, not-quite-human role because they know little or nothing about their past which would lead them to have any other opinion. Any change in their societal role may be resisted by them. A traumatic experience for many women today is the emphasis on zero-growth population. Women have been conditioned for millennia to find their identity and self-regard in motherhood. Now there is almost unanimous agreement in developed and developing countries that the two-child family must very soon become the worldwide norm or the human race will breed itself into extinction. The woman's movement for liberation with its emphasis on full personhood for women comes at a time when church and society must provide alternatives for women that are meaningful and socially rewarded in place of a life that has been child-centered, subservient, "other."

Minority groups and women must research their past and insist that it be remembered and celebrated, or they will continue to be considered an inferior "other," not to be counted as full members of the community. Also, when one is able to recognize that the group to which one belongs has been involved in significant human events, one feels a part of human experience beyond oneself. One has a sense of participation in the human community and in the making of history. One has a sense of self-esteem. Men have a sense of participation and belonging, whether in the reading of history or in the rituals of celebration. Women do not because, with the exception of the Virgin Mary in Christian liturgies, only men are named in the celebrations of praise and thanksgiving.

Why aren't women named for celebration along with Abraham, Isaac, Jacob, Moses, the prophets, the apostles, Peter and Paul and the great men of history? Why not Sarah, as well as

Abraham? Even the name of the Jews, Israelites, comes not from Abraham but from Sarah. Her name has the same root as that of Israel. Why not Miriam as well as Moses? According to the legends of the Jews it was Miriam who taught the wandering Hebrews to dig for water, to till the ground, to cultivate the tree. Why not celebrate Priscilla and Phoebe as well as Paul? Why are women—ancient and modern—excluded from history and from liturgical celebrations?

Many social as well as personal tragedies have their roots in the division of humankind into "superior" and "inferior" beings. Over and over during the long centuries Western nations, Christian people, have glorified war and sanctioned torture. Could it be that the separation of "masculine" from "feminine" qualities leading to the emphasis on aggression, physical force, military power, pride of place, and domination has led to the failure of Christians to stop the killing of the neighbor? Could it be that the ecological crisis—the wanton destruction and pollution of land, sea, air, plants, and animals—is related to a drive to dominate without the corresponding drive to nurture? Could it be that when religious sanction is given for man to hold woman, whom he loves and who loves him, in an inferior, submissive place, there are no limits to rationalizing violence toward, and exploitation of, others?

Women's liberation cannot be separated from the struggles of oppressed races because at least half of every oppressed race are women. All women and all oppressed groups share a common victimization; and there will be liberation either for all of them or for none. Human liberation is for everyone—men as well as women. It seeks to overcome the division of humankind into superior and inferior peoples which means the redressing of the imbalance of rights and of power. It seeks the end of the alienation within the individual person of feminine and masculine attributes because each attribute must be nurtured in both the female and male if a person is to be a whole person. It seeks a theology which in symbol and language will help people understand the wholeness of God and the oneness of humankind. The Spirit is moving. Human liberation waits. Tomorrow depends upon us today.

17.

The Dilemma
of Celebration

NELLE MORTON

Women appear at an impasse in celebration. Traditional symbols root too deeply in a patriarchal culture to function adequately in their new context, and new symbols have not yet emerged.[1]

The search for symbols seems to take the form of a "no-saying" and a "yes-saying" in which we see both the no and the yes as positive. We are not saying no to the whole created order of things—our traditions and ourselves included—we are saying no to those images, symbols, structures, and practices which cripple us and keep us from claiming our rightful personhood. We are saying no to a system that legitimates these images through cosmic myths, language, and daily dramas of etiquette.

We began our "no" by substituting feminine words of liturgy for those masculine words that exclude women. But soon we found that word change was not enough. The masculine words had conjured up images that continued to persist in the community psyche to proclaim gender instead of humanness. But the change provided affirmation of ourselves as persons and enabled us to hear that life is for us—directly, wholly, and lovingly. I remember once when some of us were experimenting with feminine terminology several heard, some for the first time, a word of unconditional acceptance.[2] We were not forced

---

1. Cf. Amos N. Wilder, "Theology and Theopoetic I"; "Theology and Theopoetic II"; "Theology and Theopoetic III"; *The Christian Century*, 23 May 1973; 5 December 1973; 13 March 1974.
2. Conference on "Women Exploring Theology," Grailville, Ohio, 1972 when 2 Cor. 5:17 was read ". . . for *she* is a new creation."

to make the usual transfer from the familiar masculine words to
the feminine.

Our search led beyond the sexist imagery of the biblical text
to the wholeness embedded deep within, beyond biblical history to earlier myths yielding insights that did not survive
patriarchy. Anne Bennett has already shown how *Elohim* is not
subject to gender reduction.[3] Elizabeth Gould Davis traces
Yahweh to a Sumerian goddess,[4] while Gerhard von Rad claims
any sexuality in "Jahweh" alien to Israel.[5] Others have probed
the feminine in wisdom, presence, dove, spirit, and Torah.[6]

Robert Graves's newest work describes patriarchal rejection
of woman as contributing to the decline of man,[7] and Robert Bly
inserts in his recent volume of poems a prose chapter on the
Great Mother.[8] He cites a quatrain from Job which, because of
disunity of images should read:

> I came out of the Mother naked,
> and I will be naked when I return.
> The Mother gave, and the Mother takes away,
> I love the Mother.

(The Job ending: The Lord gave, and the Lord takes away,
blessed be the name of the Lord.)

It takes little imagination to restore the creation story in
Genesis 2 to its original. The rib was womb. The patriarch's
abhorrence of blood led the Creator to allow Adam a great sleep
while fashioning a "helper fit for him." The chapter ends with
the man leaving his family and cleaving to his wife, thus clearly
matriarchal.

3. Anne McGrew Bennett, "Women in the New Society," *Journal of Current
Social Issues*, Winter 1972-73.

4. Elizabeth Gould Davis, *The First Sex* (Baltimore: G.P. Putnam's Sons, 1971),
p. 67.

5. Gerhard von Rad, *Old Testament Theology* (New York: Harper and Row,
1957), p. 146.

6. See Theodor Reik, *Pagan Rites in Judaism* (New York: Farrar, Straus and Co.,
1964), pp. 75-76; Erich Neumann, *The Great Mother*, Bollingen Series 47
(Princeton: Princeton University Press, 1955); Erminie Huntress Lantero,
Feminine Aspects of Divinity, Pendle Hill Pamphlet 191 (Wallingford, Pa.,
1973).

7. Robert Graves, *Difficult Questions, Easy Answers* (New York: Doubleday
and Co., 1974).

8. Robert Bly, *Sleepers Joining Hands* (New York: Harper and Row, 1973),
p. 31.

A comparison of John 1:1-4 with Proverbs 8:1-31 shows Word (*logos*, masculine) a substitute for wisdom (*sophia*, feminine). Since the Judeo-Christian tradition had only a patriarchal language in which to record its salvation history, and only a hierarchical perception of the universe out of which to fashion its ecclesiology, it might prove fruitful to examine some scholars' views of prepatriarchal culture. A lifetime of research has assured J. J. Bachofen that "the mythical tradition may be taken as a faithful reflection of the life of those times in which historical antiquity is rooted. It is a manifestation of primordial thinking, and immediate historical revelation, and consequently a highly reliable historical source."[9] His findings of days when the "human race has not yet . . . departed from its harmony with creation and the transcendent Creator,"[10] reveal certain similarities to today's woman experience. Primary, perhaps, is the nature of language itself, which appeared mytho-poetical in character. As language became controlled, utilitarian, and linear in patriarchal culture, metaphoric speech became reduced. In time, literal interpretations became inevitable since myth tends to literalize metaphor.

Many claim the multidimensional speech of women closer to the metaphorical than that of men.[11] If this is true, one may attribute it partly to the fact that women are more in touch with their bodies and nature in general, and also more intimately present to the symbolic of children's first speech.

Speaking organically moves near the metaphorical. Metaphor witnesses to unity between person and cosmos. Organic reflects unity between body and mind. Organic speech, then, would mean speech before the body and the spirit were split. Organic designates at-homeness in the body—the mind dipping into, and interrelated with, all the senses at their moment of sensing. The organic opens itself to mystery and wonder and

9. J. J. Bachofen, *Myth, Religion, and Mother Right* (Princeton: Princeton University Press, 1967), p. 73.

10. Ibid., p. 16.

11. Anne Schaef, psychologist, presented this view at the annual meeting of the Society for the Advancement of Continuing Education for Ministry, Denver, Colorado, June 1972; see also Helen Lynd, *On Shame and the Search for Identity* (New York: Harcourt, Brace, and Co., 1958), esp. "New Ways in Language," pp. 171-81.

awe in common aspects of life. Therefore, moments of communal ritual in prepatriarchal culture seemed to be triggered more by occasions that made the common appear of momentous import—as a birth, eating a meal, sowing seed, gathering grain, or a death. Out of physical happenings the symbolic took shape.

The ordinary word *mother* came to symbolic proportions in *Mother Earth* and then again in *Mother God.*[12] Origin from a common womb was regarded the closest possible bond and originally the only true form of kinship. When the womb came to mean the Great Womb of the Creator, the term "stranger" was not known. To injure any human being or animal was a special crime.[13] Love arising from such a bond died with the development of paternity. Mystery, the true essence of ritual, was rooted in the nature of woman and her close alliance between nature and spirit. It was thought to spring from her intimacy with death in nature and in her own body (menstruation and bleeding at childbirth). It was this mystery that evoked empathy, comfort, and raised up hope through pain.[14] The two central symbols in the cultic life of the prepatriarchal people appeared as birth and death. Birth, never completely separated from physical birth, became transparent for the whole mystery of the cosmos and creation itself. It was so with death—never bereft of its pain and its grief—but death, as birth, moved people close to the mystery of the universe.

When the knowledge of paternity, which women must have discovered first, became known to men, the men tried to usurp women's part in the birthing process. They established themselves as sole parents, reducing women to nurturing "their seed"—"their miniscule babies"—which they planted in wombs. Birth was separated from physical birth, first as an initiation rite into manhood, then sacralized into spiritual birth with men performing the functions of women.

In their ego ascendency, men contrived to beat death. They

12. Bachofen, *Myth, Religion, and Mother Right*, p. 80.
13. Davis, *The First Sex*, p. 65.
14. Bachofen, *Myth, Religion, and Mother Right*, p. 87.

would do the naming. They would have sons, and their sons' sons would have sons and thus pass on their names forever. They would amass property to pass into the hands of their sons, and their sons would add property until their ever-greater lands would compete in the whole earth. "Their seed would inherit the earth." Their tombs would be built near the hearths of their homes and their bodies moved as the sons moved, and thus they would be revered for generations and so outwit death.[15] Note how few liturgies to this day allow for grief to come full circle as a necessary part of the human experience. Modern religious structures function, as did the patriarchal, to evade death.

It is not surprising that the symbolism of birth and death from prepatriarchy became overshadowed by sexist images. In time the sexist imagery acquired a life all its own as it spun itself out in liturgy, theology, and ecclesiastical structures until the control group became unable to perceive the distortions in the life of the community.

The patriarchal effort to suppress the feminine in Judeo-Christian history was never completely accomplished. In times of greatest harmony and peace, of hope and vision, the feminine surfaced to approximate a mutuality and balance in the community. Even though the covenant community excluded women in their primary membership, women were never entirely silenced.

Perhaps modern women experience birth and death similarly to the prepatriarchal rites. The following excerpts from accounts of a birth and a death support such a theory.

The persons present at the birth (including several seminary graduates) had, at one time or another, lived together under one roof, sharing food and work, pain and joy, strengthening one another's days, and hearing one another's anger. By right of having lived together in this fashion they considered themselves a family, and as family, belonged to be present at the advent of the new member who was loved before she was born.

---

15. See Fustel de Coulanges, *The Ancient City* (Boston: Lee and Shepherd, 1925).

Susie gave birth to Leila . . . but many helped. I suppose there
were twenty-five present . . . mostly women. Two children
wandered in and out among us . . . 3-year-old Blake said: "She
popped out." Safra, Leila's sister asked, "Is she my baby?"
Soon after she said she was Leila's mommy.

* * * *

Three women nurses or midwives were there. . . . One
helped lift Leila out when the time came. . . . The doctor, like
God, walked in and out with his suit and tie; his knowledge
and his authority. He affirmed that Susie was in transition. He
did not know any of us. He walked out again. I was glad he did
not stay.

* * * *

At a low time when we thought Susie might have to leave
her friends for the hospital Mariette felt she wanted to pray.
But she said she fought that off because she knew we have to
find inside ourselves how to get through.

Joe breathed with Susie through her contractions . . . he
stayed by her side most of those 18 hours. . . . Some women
knelt on either side rubbing her feet and legs or forehead . . .
watching for any place she began to tense . . . getting her
ice . . . talking with her between contractions. In general
people were quiet. . . . We weren't trying not to speak. . . . It
was just a time of great emotion.

Someone made chicken soup, which Susie had requested.
All were relaxed until the pushing began and we knew the
baby was coming. When Susie began pushing, her face
strained . . . got red . . . everyone held their breaths and
pushed with her. The pushing felt good. It was exciting because the baby was finally going to come. Even though in
great pain Susie's face was smiling. . . . Susie pushed. . . . We
all pushed for about 3 to 5 minutes . . . then the baby's head
showed.

* * * *

Leila did almost pop out. She cried immediately. . . . At
first she was white . . . then turned pink slowly. . . . She
smelled good. When Leila cried everyone in the room cried
too. . . . We hugged and kissed one another. Someone laid
Leila across Susie's breasts. She nursed. A nurse helped get

the placenta out . . . Joe cut the cord. Leila cried some more. In an hour or so Susie got up and sat in a rocker in the sunshine with Leila. . . . Friends went out and cooked the biggest dinner of all that night. . . . It seemed that Leila had come to all of us. Later we talked of the overwhelming awe. The birth was life-giving.[16]

In the death account the father, mother, and sister sat in a front pew during the service for their four-year-old who had been killed by a driver under the influence of drugs. One minister provided traditional prayers and structure. Another told stories out of the life of the little girl, now dead. Still another, a woman, assigned to read the Scripture, began:

> How could a service such as this have begun with a hymn of praise? How could we sing together out of the strange happening in our midst?
> Long ago a psalmist (Ps. 22) struggled with similar questions. O God, Our God, why have you forsaken us? Why are you so far from hearing us, so far from the world of our anguish and our anger? We cry out by day but you do not answer. We cry out in the night but find no rest. . . . After his anger the psalmist cried: O Lord, be not longer so far off. You are our help. Hasten to our aid. He ended with a paean of praise introduced by the telling phrase, In the midst of the congregation we can praise.
> Here emerged a clue to the answer of our questions. . . . In the midst of the human community of faith, singing is possible . . . before the anguish is over. Praise is possible before the fact . . . before the joy and meaning are fully known.
> In the midst of this congregation gathered, with so much love, to support and sustain you, Joyce, and Debbie, and Bob . . . grace may communicate itself to you even while it is yet dark. No . . . because it is dark.
> Matthew (18:1-4), too, speaks of a congregation . . . the nucleus of the church-to-be. The disciples had been vying with one another as to which of them would be most important in the ecclesiastical hierarchy, so they brought their question to Jesus. And Jesus called a little child, like Susan, and put the child in the midst of them. Then he said to the men: Unless you turn and become

16. Condensed from a long account by Judy Davis (staff member of the Institute for Policy Studies, Washington, D.C.). Used by permission.

like a child you will never enter the kingdom of heaven.
. . . Whoever can become like this child, that one is
greatest.
If this be true, then children belong as congregation . . . not as
objects to be ministered to or potential adults to be indoctri-
nated . . . but as persons in their own right to minister to us all.
And if this be true, Susan's so short life was ministry indeed.[17]

There was recognition throughout the days of mourning that
grief belongs at such a time. Friends and family affirmed the
living. They allowed for the joy before it became a reality. But
they could not predate the celebration, for it had already begun
to take place.

In the light of our tradition, our experiences as women provide a clue to the structure of a new symbol. We do not look up
and out for our story as we have been conditioned to do all our
lives. We touch the pain in our own lives to find it derives from
false images imposed upon us.

Once we took the painful journey to the core of our lives, we
found that we were sustained. In the awful loneliness we were
not alone. Something shaped our cry—brought forth our
speech, fragmentary as it was. We had been told all our lives
that the word created, that the word came first—even in the
beginning, before the beginning. Now we know a priority to
the word—a hearing that brought forth the word. We literally
heard one another down to a word that was *our* word, and that
word was ourselves.

Hearing, as we have come to experience it, proceeds not from
a collective ear that would suggest an aggregate, but from a
great ear at the heart of the universe hearing persons to humanness. And the humanness is marked by wholeness (the whole
word, and not just the masculine word). In the morphology
—down, then up from down under—we have experienced
birth, not rebirth, not new birth, or rite of passage or entry, but
birth of ourselves for the first time. We have experienced creation, not re-creation, or new creation, but a primordial creation
of ourselves. In the new shape of our experience we have

17. Book on the death of Susan Clark (1973), daughter of the Rev. and Mrs.
Robert Clark, Madison, N.J., now in the process of being written.

confronted death, but not death of the self, or death to self. We have experienced the death of the stereotyped images, the breaking of them from within so that self can be affirmed and potentialized. No one can take this journey of women but the women themselves who are involved. To put it on "Jesus," or the priest, or the therapist is to perpetuate the same dependency we are now seeking to throw off.

One can only speculate on what celebration could be were mutuality (love) possible in the community of faith; were the oppressed of the earth trusted to become a valid part of that community.

It may be that the most authentic celebration is not that which can be structured from above—not that as considered by the control group proper for the oppressed, nor as some would have us believe—Dionysian (induced). Maybe the most authentic celebration begins with rejoicing in that which is breaking up from down under.

Contributors

ANNE McGREW BENNETT has a Master's degree in Religious Education from Auburn Theological Seminary (1932). She has long been active in the peace movement and women's liberation, serving on the board of the Office of Women's Affairs (G.T.U.) since its inception in 1970. Among her writings is "Women in the New Society," *The Journal of Current Social Issues*, Winter 1972-73.

KAREN L. BLOOMQUIST is an M.Div. graduate (1974) of the Pacific Lutheran Theological Seminary, Berkeley, and is pursuing a call to the parish ministry of the American Lutheran church. She is active in the promotion of woman's role in her denomination, and has served as both a staff member and board member of the Office of Women's Affairs (G.T.U.).

BETSY BRENNEMAN holds a B.A. in English from Denison University, Ohio, and is an M.A. student of philosophical theology at the G.T.U. She has been a member of the staff of the Office of Women's Affairs (G.T.U.), and on the editorial staff of the journal *Radical Religion*. Ms. Brenneman was associated with the Swallow Press, Chicago, as Assistant to the Editor.

KATHLEEN BREWER received an M.A. and M.Div. from the Pacific School of Religion, Berkeley, in 1974. She is an artist, and was a staff member of the Office of Women's Affairs (G.T.U.) for two years. She is an ordained minister of the Christian church (Disciples of Christ).

ERDMUT MUELLER BROWN is a native of Germany who has worked professionally for the World Council of Churches and the Lutheran World Federation. She is presently teaching French and German in Berkeley. She secured a translator's degree from the University of Geneva, Switzerland, and an M.A. in Education from North Michigan University. She is a board member of the Office of Women's Affairs (G.T.U.).

DOROTHY DONNELLY is the Chairperson of the National Coalition of American Nuns and a member of the faculty of the Jesuit School of Theology in Berkeley. She received a Ph.D. in Classics from the

128

Catholic University and a Th.D. from the Graduate Theological Union. Two of her books have been published thus far (*St. Thomas More's Answer to Luther* and *The Sister Apostle*), and a third on women and prisons is being prepared for publication.

PAT DRISCOLL received her B.A. in Fine Arts from the University of California, Berkeley. She has used her artistic and writing talent in both parish level and ecumenical activities. Her workshops for Christian women have been highly successful.

CLARE BENEDICKS FISCHER is a Ph.D. candidate in the sociology of religion at the Graduate Theological Union. Her doctoral thesis is concerned with a feminist approach to the theology of work. In addition to her staff involvement in the Office of Women's Affairs (G.T.U.), she has served as an editor of the "Women's Caucus—Religious Studies Newsletter."

KATHY JAN JOHNSON is an M.Div. student of the American Baptist Seminary of the West, Berkeley, and is working toward ordination to the ministry of the American Baptist church. She is involved in an internship at the denomination's national headquarters in Valley Forge, Pennsylvania, and is a representative to the National Council of Churches Assembly. She has served on the staff of the Office of Women's Affairs (G.T.U.).

KAREN LEBACQZ has completed her studies in Christian Ethics for the Ph.D. at Harvard University. She is a member of the faculty of the Pacific School of Religion with a speciality in medical ethics. She is also a member of the board of the Office of Women's Affairs (G.T.U.).

JACQUELINE MEADOWS received an M.A. in Religious Education from the Pacific School of Religion in 1961, and an M.Div. from the same institution in 1974. She is an ordained deacon and serves as minister to a Methodist church in the Bay Area while she continues her studies at the Graduate Theological Union for a Ph.D. in Religion and the Arts.

NELLE MORTON is Associate Professor Emeritus of the theological school, Drew University. She has taught and lectured widely at a number of theological institutions including Harvard Divinity School, Union Theological Seminary (N.Y.), and the Graduate Theological Union. Her interest in language and women's liberation is represented in a number of articles.

LINDA MOYER has an M.A. in French from Middlebury College. She is a free-lance writer who has served on the editorial staff of the journal

Radical Religion since its creation. She is currently at work on a project dealing with socialism and the women's movement.

CAROL NESS is a staff member of the Ecumenical Peace Institute and active with the American Friends Service Committee. She has a B.A. in Sociology from the University of Washington and serves as a member of the board of the Office of Women's Affairs (G.T.U.).

CLAIRE RANDALL is the General Secretary of the National Council of the Churches of Christ in the United States of America. Before coming to that position she was the Associate Executive Director of Church Women United. She has been a spokesperson for women's liberation within the church for many years.

DOROTHEE SOELLE obtained her Ph.D. in philology and theology at the University of Freiburg and Goettingen, in Germany. She is on the faculty of the Institute of Germanic Philology at the University of Cologne and active in the work of Christians for Socialism. Among her published books translated into English are: *Christ the Representative: An Essay in Theology after the Death of God* (Fortress Press, 1967), *Political Theology* (Fortress Press, 1974), and *Suffering* (to be published by Fortress Press).

BARBARA B. TROXELL received her M.Div. from Union Theological Seminary in New York and was ordained through the United Methodist Church: deacon in 1958, elder in 1961. She is currently an Associate Pastor of the First Presbyterian Church (Palo Alto, California) and instructs a class in feminist theology at California State University, San Jose.

CAROL VALAKAI is completing her studies for the M.Div. at the Pacific Lutheran Theological Seminary, Berkeley. She is serving as an intern in a local parish in Phoenix, Arizona. During her years in Berkeley she was active on the board of the Ecumenical Peace Institute, the peace caucus of the Graduate Theological Union, and the staff of the Office of Women's Affairs (G.T.U.).

Suggested Readings and Resources

BIBLIOGRAPHIES

Cisler, Lucinda. "Women: A Bibliography." Xeroxed. Available from author, 50¢ prepaid: 102 W. 80 St., New York, N.Y. 10024.

Farians, Elizabeth. "Selected Bibliography on Women and Religion." Mimeographed. Available from author, 75¢ prepaid: 6125 Webbland Place, Cincinnati, Ohio 45213.

Fischer, Clare B. "Woman: A Theological Perspective." Xeroxed. Available from Office of Women's Affairs of the Graduate Theological Union, $2.00 prepaid: 2465 Le Conte Ave., Berkeley, Calif. 94709.

O'Connor, Patricia. *Women: A Selected Bibliography.* Springfield, Ohio: Wittenberg University. Available, $2.00 prepaid.

SPECIAL ISSUES

Andover-Newton Quarterly 12 (March 1972). Special issue on women's liberation and theology, including articles by Mary Daly, Nelle Morton, etc.

Annals of the New York Academy of Sciences (Article 3) 175 (1970): 781-1065. "The Impact of Fertility Limitation on Women's Life-Career and Personality." Edited by Esther Milner.

Chicago Theological Seminary Register 60, no. 3 (March 1970). "Woman."

Dialog 10, Spring 1971. "The Church and Women's Liberation."

Lutheran Quarterly 24, no. 1 (February 1972). "Essays by Laywomen."

Reflection 69, May 1972. Articles by women at Yale Divinity School on church and theology.

Risk 7, no. 1 (1971). "Gladly We Rebel." Publication of World Council of Churches.

Social Action 37, no. 8 (April 1971). "Women in Church and Society." Publication of United Church of Christ.

Soundings 53, no. 4 (Winter 1970). "Women's Liberation and the Theologians." Includes Krister Stendahl and Rosemary R. Ruether.

Theological Education 8 (Summer 1972). "Women in Theological Education: Past, Present, and Future."

131

Women and Religion—1972; Women and Religion—1973: Proceedings of the Working Group on Women and Religion. Missoula, Mont.: American Academy of Religion.

BOOKS

Bernard, Jessie. *The Future of Marriage.* New York: World Publishing Co., 1972.

Carothers, J. Edward; Mead, Margaret; McCracken, Daniel D.; Shinn, Roger, eds. *To Love or To Perish: The Technological Crisis and the Churches.* New York: Friendship Press, 1972.

Crook, Margaret B. *Women and Religion.* Boston: Beacon Press, 1964.

Culver, Elsie T. *Women in the World of Religion.* Garden City, N.Y.: Doubleday and Co., 1967.

Daly, Mary. *The Church and the Second Sex.* New York: Harper and Row, 1968.

———. *Beyond God the Father.* Boston: Beacon Press, 1974.

Doely, Sarah Bentley, ed. *Women's Liberation and the Church.* New York: Association Press, 1970.

Emswiler, Sharon Neufer, and Emswiler, Thomas Neufer. *Women and Worship: A Guide to Non-Sexist Hymns, Prayers and Liturgies.* New York: Harper and Row, 1974.

Ermath, Margaret. *Adam's Fractured Rib.* Philadelphia: Fortress Press, 1970.

Figes, Eva. *Patriarchal Attitudes.* New York: Stein and Day, 1970.

Gilman, Charlotte Perkins. *Women and Economics.* New York: Harper and Row, 1966.

Goode, William J. *Women in Divorce.* New York: Free Press, 1956.

Janeway, Elizabeth. *Man's World—Woman's Place: A Study of Social Mythology.* New York: William Morrow, 1971.

Morris, Joan. *The Lady Was a Bishop: The Hidden History of Women with Clerical Ordination and the Jurisdiction of Bishops.* New York: Macmillan Co., 1973.

Myrdal, Alva, and Klein, Viola. *Women's Two Roles, Home and Work.* London: Routledge and Kegan Paul, 1968.

O'Brien, Patricia. *The Woman Alone.* New York: Quadrangle Press, 1973.

Ruether, Rosemary R., ed. *Religion and Sexism.* New York: Simon and Schuster, 1974.

Stendahl, Krister. *The Bible and the Role of Women: A Case Study in Hermeneutics.* Philadelphia: Fortress Press, 1966.

Swidler, Arlene, ed. *Sistercelebrations: Nine Worship Experiences.* Philadelphia: Fortress Press, 1974.

Tavard, George. *Women in Christian Tradition.* Notre Dame: University of Notre Dame Press, 1973.

Taves, Isabella. *Women Alone.* New York: Funk and Wagnalls, 1968.